PRAISE FOR RELATIONSHIP SOLUTIONS

"Relationship Solutions is one of the most effective books about relationships (and living) I have ever read. It addresses one of the deepest, most personal topics in clear, simple terms, and puts the focus on success exactly where it belongs; with the reader. For people facing conflict in their marriage, this book has the power to transform by helping readers look inside themselves for the real answers. As someone who has worked with divorcing families for more than thirty years, I am eager to give this out to everyone who is facing this difficult situation. It covers the full spectrum of relationship decisions, from the decision about divorce, to the ways of going through divorce, to the journey after divorce with exceptional clarity and insight."

—Ronald D. Ousky, Esq.
Author of *The Collaborative Way to Divorce:*
The Revolutionary Method that Results in Less Stress,
Lower Costs and Happier Kids--Without Going to Court

"Relationship Solutions is a great resource for anybody considering divorce, going through a divorce, or recently divorced."

—Dan Couvrette
CEO, DivorceMag.com, DivorcedMoms.com,
FamilyLawyerMagazine.com

Relationship
Solutions

*Effective Strategies to
Heal Your Heart and Create
the Happiness You Deserve*

BY SONIA FRONTERA

Coventina House
71 North Franklin Street
Lambertville, NJ 08530

Relationship Solutions: Effective Strategies to Heal Your Heart and Create the Happiness You Deserve
Copyright© 2020 by Sonia Frontera

Coventina House books are available at a discount when purchased in quantity for promotional or corporate use. Special editions, which include personalized covers, excerpts and corporate imprints can be customized for large purchases. For additional information, call (908) 996-4219 or email media@soniafrontera.com.

ISBN 978-1-7335695-4-5 (Paperback)
ISBN 978-1-7335695-5-2 (Ebook)

Printed in the United States of America
Editor: Connie Wilson

Cover design: Mariah Sinclair
Book design: Vincent Saldana

Publisher's Cataloging-In-Publication Data
(Prepared by The Donohue Group, Inc.)

Names: Frontera, Sonia, author.
Title: Relationship solutions : effective strategies to heal your heart and create the happiness you deserve / by Sonia Frontera.
Description: Lambertville, NJ : Coventina House, [2020] | Series: [The sister's guides to empowered living] ; [3] | Includes bibliographical references.
Identifiers: ISBN 9781733569545 (paperback) | ISBN 9781733569552 (ebook)
Subjects: LCSH: Marriage--Psychological aspects--Popular works. | Marital conflict--Popular works. | Interpersonal relations--Popular works. | Divorce--Popular works. | LCGFT: Self-help publications.
Classification: LCC HQ734 .F76 2020 (print) | LCC HQ734 (ebook) | DDC 646.7/82--dc23

Disclaimer

This book contains the opinions and ideas of its author. It is intended to provide helpful and informative material on the subjects addressed in the book. It is sold with the understanding that the author and publisher are not engaged in rendering medical, health, legal or any other kind of professional services in this book.

The reader should consult his or her medical, health, legal or other competent professional before adopting any of the suggestions in this book or drawing inferences from it. The author and publisher specifically disclaim any and all responsibility for any liability, loss, or risk, personal or otherwise, which is incurred as a consequence, directly or indirectly, of the use and application of any of the contents of this book.

Table of Contents

PART III
KEEPING THINGS AMICABLE. **139**

PART IV
POWERING UP FOR A GRACIOUS EXIT **187**

PART V
CREATING THE HAPPINESS YOU DESERVE. . . 251

Dear Reader

YOU have the power to heal your heart and create the joyful life you deserve.

If you're reading these pages, you are probably unhappily married, and the thought of divorce has crossed or, quite possibly, consumed your mind.

Perhaps you feel miserable in your marriage and are craving more satisfaction and joy in your life.

Or you are pondering the devastating decision whether to leave your spouse or to stay.

Maybe your spouse just dropped the "D Bomb," and you feel heartbroken, disoriented and confused, wondering, "Where did the love go and where do I go from here?"

You may be in the midst of a divorce by choice or default, and are seeking comfort, guidance and support.

If any of the above statements apply to you, *this book is for you.*

I have fantastic news! While divorce is an unnerving experience, there's light at the end of the tunnel.

I have been through the tunnel myself and can assure you that you can get through it. I will help you along the way, so you can come out on the other side, stronger and wiser than when you tied the knot. In fact, I have a secret for you… YOU possess the inner light to shine the way through the divorce tunnel.

I realize you're in pain and I am not minimizing it. I have experienced the pain of divorce in the flesh. I'm very familiar with it.

Perhaps the thought of divorcing seems surreal. The sort of thing you never expected could happen to you.

Nobody gets married intending to get divorced. We all go to the altar—or the beach, or the gazebo—full of hopes and dreams, intending to live happily ever after. Sadly, divorce is a reality for *at least* 40% of married couples—the 40% who do divorce plus those unaccounted for, who silently suffer in excruciating marriages, unable to get out.

For some, it is the result of a major event, like infidelity. For others, it is death by a thousand cuts—the result of a lot of thought, hesitation, ambivalence and fear.

Perhaps your spouse asked you for a divorce, seemingly out of nowhere, and you feel blindsided and confused.

It doesn't matter who leaves whom or whether one of the parties has already hooked up with somebody else. The end of a marriage is like the death of a loved one. It inevitably involves grieving and a deep sense of loss.

It happened to me…

Having been unhappily married myself, and through my work with divorcing couples and women hurting in abusive relationships, I understand your desire to end the pain—for good. To find the strength, the wisdom and the courage to take action, to figure out—and carry out—what's right for you.

When I was in your shoes, there were few books about troubled relationships. While these books delivered insightful information, they generally focused on the psychology of relationships. And those written for female readers, mostly dissected the dysfunctional behaviors of men. They did not offer the comfort I needed to heal my pain, nor helped me chart the next steps, nor empowered me to carry them out.

That's why I have written this book for you—*as a supportive sister* who cares. It is my intention to provide you with a roadmap and to empower you on your journey of personal transformation. It is my vow to help you get clear, get strong and end the pain you are feeling in your marriage—whether you repair it or you let it go—so you can enjoy the magnificent life you deserve.

The purpose of this book is to guide you, whether you're unhappily married or involuntarily separated, to heal your broken heart and create the happiness you deserve.

This book contemplates two possible scenarios:

1) Divorce is averted, and the parties overcome their differences resurrecting their marriage and ending with a healthier relationship than when the crisis began; or

2) The parties divorce amicably and move on to enjoy fulfilling lives separately—smarter and more satisfied than when they said, "I do."

I can't promise you that your marriage will repair itself and you and your spouse will ride together into the sunset on a white stallion. But I can assure you that marital problems and the divorce process itself can be vehicles for personal growth and can blaze a trail to unexpected happiness.

That is my truth, and I'm here to share the shortcuts.

Consider reading this book as an empowering adventure with a loving sister who has been to hell and back, and will take you by the hand and cheer you on as you mend your broken heart and reinvent yourself into the fulfilled person you are meant to be.

I will share practical strategies to guide you as you make the daunting decision whether to stay in your relationship (as a wiser, empowered YOU) or to end your marriage with serenity and grace, and to confidently *create* a new life from the inside out.

I did it, and YOU can, too!

Together, we will embark on a journey of self-discovery, to gain clarity and fortify your spirit, culminating in creating consciously.

By the time you finish this book—and do the exercises in it—you will:

Get Clear

- Practice active awareness to discover the traps that may have lured you into an unhappy marriage, so you can avoid repeating the same mistakes in the future.

- Explore the negative beliefs and attitudes that trap you in unsatisfying relationships and master strategies to dissolve them.

- Examine your marital dynamics, so you can understand what you need from a marriage.

- Assess how your relationship measures up to your needs and whether you and your spouse can build a satisfying life together.

- Find out if you're in an abusive relationship and tap into resources for ending your marriage safely.

- Make peace with your past choices and their consequences and allow a future of unlimited possibility.

- Decide whether to leave your marriage or to stay.

If your marriage isn't viable and you're on the divorce path, this book will help you:

Get Strong

- Prepare for the divorce journey.
- Build your support team.
- Become your own best friend.
- Cultivate self-love practices to nurture your mind, body and spirit.
- Improve self-esteem.
- Conquer stress and maintain productivity.
- Dissolve the fears that paralyze you.

Move On
- Develop your exit strategy.
- Learn strategies to keep your divorce cordial.
- Create your life intentionally from the inside out.
- Move on with confidence and self-reliance.

How to Use This Book

I recommend you give this book one quick read first. Get familiar with the concepts and techniques. Then revisit every section with care and reflect on its contents. Read all the sections and complete all the exercises, even if you think they do not apply to you.

Whether you are wondering if divorce is right for you or if you're already on the divorce path, these insights and reflections will help you understand how you ended up in relationship hell. They will provide insights not only into your own thought patterns, but may shed light on your spouse's mindset as well. These sections will help you identify problems in your relationship and trace their origins. Moreover, the strategies outlined in this book will help you identify harmful emotional programming and prevent you from repeating similar mistakes in the future.

I advise you to keep a journal to memorialize your thoughts and gather them together in one place. I also suggest that you make entries on your journal daily to document other revelations and feelings. Revisit your writings often and keep track of your progress.

Adopt active awareness and apply the strategies in this book as a way of life, so you can create the joyful life you deserve.

Congratulate yourself for every baby step accomplished and get ready to write a new story!

You Deserve to Be Happy!

Thank you for allowing me to be your traveling companion on your personal journey. I promise it will be eye-opening and exhilarating. Like you, I was once unhappily married, and I understand what you are going through. I understand the horror of waking up next to a person you no longer know.

I tormented myself with self-blame for missing the red flags that should have alerted me to an imminent mistake. I also endured the insanity of hanging on to an unsalvageable marriage, and the heartache of not being able to keep alive what initially had meant so much to me.

Like some of you, I was also on the fence—for years. I know the disappointment, the ambivalence and the fear of the unknown. I have felt the loss of my dearest dreams and the isolation of not being understood.

But my story also has a happy ending. I triumphed over marital adversity, and as a result of this disastrous relationship, experienced unimaginable personal growth. I have also come to treasure freedom and happiness as my birthrights—birthrights *no one can take away from me.*

Here's the basic premise of this journey. No matter your age, your background, or what you've been through in life, you deserve to be happy. And you can create the happiness you deserve.

You may not be experiencing the happiness you deserve in your marriage at this time. We enter marriage expecting it will make us happy, but oftentimes marriage turns out to be a source of disappointment and grief.

Come to the realization that nobody is responsible for making you happy. Happiness is a state of mind. It is an inside job that no one else can do for you. As you do the exercises in this book, you will learn to examine your relationship with your partner, explore what led to strife in the relationship, and own responsibility for the happiness that is yours for the taking.

Once you accept that your happiness is nobody's business but your own, you will feel empowered to adopt new strategies and transform yourself from a victim to an active participant in your personal happiness project. You will break free from the prison of blame and enter into the sanctuary of freedom. You will embrace habits and nurturing practices that will restore a sense of fulfillment in your life. And you will be excited to create your future.

Life may look bleak right now but take heart. You have before you a unique opportunity to start over, to reinvent yourself, to be happy again—confident and smarter than ever before. *With or without your spouse.*

I got through it all, and so can you! It is my sincere desire that you find the peace, the joy and the freedom that await you on the other side.

Brace yourself for the adventure of your life!

PART I

GET CLEAR

Breaking the Spell

If you are wondering whether you married the wrong person, or how you ended up marrying the wrong person, congratulate yourself! You're on the right track. Looks like you're ready to wake up!

Psychotherapist, author and spiritual teacher, Anthony de Mello, S.J., said most people don't know it, but they are born asleep, live asleep, marry in their sleep, and die in their sleep without ever waking up. This statement, while shocking, makes perfect sense. It encapsulates the key reasons we live unsatisfying lives and *get in* and *stay in* unhappy marriages.

De Mello blamed our social programing and maintained that awareness, "waking up," offered the way out of our suffering. Think about it... We are conditioned to live under a spell. The roadmap for our journey in this world comes from our authority figures: parents, teachers and social institutions like the church, the media, advertising. We inherit our beliefs, our religion, our fears and prejudices, political affiliation—pretty much our whole make up—from our families and communities. We have assimilated society's ideas and behavioral norms without question and have come to accept them as our own.

This lack of awareness often gets us into trouble. Many of us live unexamined lives, following the footsteps of our parents and their parents, perpetuating generations of mindlessness. We go through life on autopilot, obediently following the course laid out for us.

We are trained to graduate high school, go to college, get a job, get married, have kids, work for 40 years, retire and die.

Our programming also includes a list of marital rules, things like the right timing (you don't want to be a spinster/bachelor), what kind of spouse is acceptable (someone from your race, religion or social class), how to interact with our spouses (men wear the pants), and how to raise our children (children need both parents to be happy).

As a result, we often make major decisions without reflection, not recognizing the factors that influenced our choices, while social forces operate surreptitiously in the background.

No wonder we marry the wrong person, at the wrong time, pursue the wrong profession—or fail to pursue our fondest dreams. Then one day we find ourselves miserably unhappy but have no idea why. After all, we played by the rules and did what we were supposed to do!

So we end up feeling stuck in unfulfilling lives because we think that's as good as it gets. We don't realize that we are not living our own lives but lives that have been prepackaged for us and may not suit us. And, unfortunately, "the package" doesn't include the tools to help us dig ourselves out.

The antidote to this poison? Active awareness. Awareness breaks the spell. Awareness sets us free. With an aware mindset, you will no longer accept a life that is prepackaged by others.

You may feel imprisoned because you married the wrong person and are paying the steep price of a sequence of wrong choices. But rather than defaulting into blame, you will use active awareness to understand how you got in this mess. You will take responsibility for the choices you made and consciously decide how to repair the effects of your poor choices. You will seize the power to bounce back and plot your next moves.

With the application of active awareness, you will *create* your life intentionally and deliciously! You will step out of your role as an obedient member of the clan and embrace a life in which you always have a choice and create from *your* conscious choices. I am going to repeat that: *you always have a choice!*

You can choose what you do, how you feel, and how you respond to circumstances and events. And if you make a wrong choice, it's okay. Instead of beating yourself up, I invite you to pick yourself up, examine your mistakes, own them, and learn from them. And then *you can choose again.*

You get a fresh start with every choice. You get to choose the life you want. You get to decide *what's in it and who's in it*— your spouse, friends, family, enjoyable activities and rewarding work. In other words, you exercise your choice to create a life of freedom and fulfillment.

Awareness is like a muscle. In the beginning, it can be weak and atrophied. But with steady practice, it can become strong and carry you in every situation.

As you go through the exercises in this book, you will begin to use active awareness as a power tool until it becomes second nature. You will learn to live an examined life and how to respond to every situation—even trying ones—from an awakened place. You will recognize your option to feel serene and in control. You will cultivate the skills to turn obstacles into opportunities to create the happiness you deserve.

Active Awareness: The Art of Personal Observation

Strengthening the Awareness Muscle - An Introduction to Mindful Living

Are you ready to experience freedom and fulfillment? Are you excited to *create* your life intentionally?

Before we begin our journey of self-discovery, healing and conscious creation, let me explain what I mean by active awareness. Then you can understand how to apply it in your life.

First, you will use it to uncover how you ended up in an unsatisfying marriage, and second, to help you *get out* and *stay out* of the traps you will probably encounter in the future. Finally, you can implement active awareness to create a joyful life going forward.

Active awareness is snapping out of the spell. It is turning off the autopilot and getting behind the wheel. It is the renunciation of the mindlessness of everyday life.

You may have heard the term mindfulness a lot. It is kind of fashionable. You may have seen advertisements for mindfulness classes and seen lots of books about mindfulness. This is all great stuff, but it may have given you the impression that mindfulness is mysterious and complicated—as something that requires going to school.

But what I propose here is way simpler and easy to implement. It is meant to initiate you in mindful, aware living with simple techniques, so you can get started and run with it.

As I define it, active awareness is the art of personal observation. A commitment to paying attention to your thoughts and actions. Being on the lookout. Always. No matter where you are. No matter what you're doing.

It means liberating yourself from living mindlessly day in and day out and dissolving the influence of background forces.

It consists of catching yourself when your mind turns on the autopilot switch and takes you for a spin on crazy-thought highway.

It is waking up and getting back on track.

You may resist, saying to yourself, "That's crazy! I am not mindless!" Think about it. How many times have you opened a bag of potato chips, and before you knew it, they were all gone? And the only evidence that *you* ate them is that you feel stuffed with guilt? How many times have you been introduced to another person and, by the end of the conversation, you can't remember his or her name?

I am guilty of both. And this mindlessness spills into many areas of your life, obviously unbeknownst to you.

Mindlessness also happens to be the mother of insane thinking. Do you ever find yourself sliding in an avalanche of unstoppable catastrophic thoughts? It starts with a fight with your spouse over something stupid, and you end your story living under a bridge?

I know you do. We *all* do.

As we discussed earlier, you probably fell into the trap of an unsuitable marriage because you were cruising on autopilot. You were not engaging in self-reflection. You were going through the motions without thinking, most likely because of hidden feelings and social forces. Or you stay trapped in your marriage because you torment yourself with thoughts that steal your peace and disempower you. Or you act without thinking and react to unpleasant situations saying and doing things you later regret.

But you don't have to live that way. When you practice active awareness, you embrace the habit of staying in the present, where everything happens, and where you can do something about it. You have the choice to be in the now, where change can take place and solutions flow, rather than in the past, stewing over old hurts, or in the future, worrying about who gets the house or the holiday schedule with the kids.

Life is meant to be delicious! Imagine the joy of savoring every minute and exerting complete control over your thoughts and feelings. Consider owning your power to keep out negative thoughts about your spouse, dissolving feelings of self-loathing and erasing revenge fantasies, catching yourself before your actions and reactions get you into trouble.

Imagine being able to live with a clear mind and connecting with the inner sage that guides you to make the right decisions at every fork in the road. This is what active awareness will do for you.

In future chapters I will guide you through a series of reflections that will provide you with a roadmap to uncover the destructive thought patterns and thoughtless behaviors that got you into an unhappy marriage. These reflections will bring awareness to the process that led you to your past choices and will help you keep awareness in the forefront. That way, you will avoid repeating past mistakes, so you can rebuild your life the way you want it—and from a position of clarity and power, to boot!

Let's put an end to mindlessness and begin living consciously. We will start with the following two exercises. They are simple hacks that, when practiced daily, will strengthen your awareness muscle and help you cultivate the art of personal observation. Do them in conjunction with the exercises and written reflections you will find throughout this book.

Exercise 1
60-60-30 Spell SNAP

This exercise is designed to help you catch yourself in mindless or obsessive thinking and to SNAP out of the spell! Next, you return your awareness to the present moment.

This is how it goes...

> S - Stop.
> N - Notice.
> A - Analyze your thoughts and feelings.
> P - Return to the present moment.

Set an alarm on your phone or watch to go off every 60 minutes during your waking hours. A cheap digital watch that you can keep in your purse or pocket is perfect. When you hear the alarm, stop for 60 seconds and answer the following questions:

> *Where am I now?*
> *What am I doing?*
> *What am I thinking?*
> *Where is this thought coming from?*
> *What am I feeling? Why?*
> *Am I at peace?*

The simple act of stopping will help you break existing mindlessness patterns and will incite you to act consciously. You can add to your inquiry:

What brought me here?
What is this moment teaching me?
What do I choose to create from this moment?

Examine your answers with curiosity and without judgment and try to spot any lessons they may contain.

As you continue to practice this exercise, you will notice how frequently you are under the spell without realizing it. And you will develop the habit of consciously returning your focus to your surroundings and the task at hand.

When the alarm goes off, you may be surprised by the realization that you are re-living in your head an argument with your spouse, catastrophizing about losing your job or agonizing over a presentation you are making tomorrow. Or you may be lost in reverie while your food is burning on the stove.

The possible scripts are endless. But you get my point. While caught under the spell, you may be missing a spectacular sunset, or a valuable insight or idea, or a special moment with a loved one. Simply put, you are missing out on life!

Do this exercise every 60 minutes, for 60 seconds, for at least 30 days, enough time to create a new habit. You can also use this exercise when you are feeling tense or anxious or when you are on the brink of an unpleasant situation.

At the end of the 30 days, you will find it easier to detect when you become spellbound, without the alarm even sounding off!

Exercise 2
Put Your Crazy Thoughts on Trial

Thoughts are the building blocks of our experience. Much of the misery we inflict on ourselves is the result of out-of-control thinking. You are the boss of your mind, even if it appears to be the other way around. Here's a dirty trick from my trial lawyer days you can successfully apply to stop obsessive thinking.

At trial, attorneys make objections to keep their adversaries' evidence out. You have seen this on TV and in the movies. They also use them to break the other lawyer's train of thought (though it's not a nice thing to do).

Derail your train of negative thoughts! When you catch yourself entertaining crazy thoughts, say to yourself, "Objection!" and interrupt your thinking.

Take this a step further. Analyze the insanity of your thoughts, and place valid trial objections on your mental record.

How about?

- Irrelevant.
- Speculative.
- Assuming facts not in evidence.
- Hearsay.
- Repetitive.
- Argumentative.
- Confusing, misleading, unintelligible.

Give thought to your thoughts and recognize how they sentence you to pain and suffering. By bringing awareness to your thinking patterns, you will snap out of the spell and open the way to achieving clarity.

Ditching Negative Thought Patterns and Adopting a Success Mindset

One of the most insidious social programs inflicted on us is labeling marital breakdown as a failure. I don't want you to fall for that.

In a perfect world, you and your spouse may work out your differences, resurrect your marriage and emerge stronger than ever before. It can happen to you, and the exercises in this book may help you do just that.

In the real world, however, that's not always the case. Couples sometimes grow apart; their differences accentuate and there are hurts too deep to overcome. Divorce, then, becomes inevitable. But is it a failure? Does it make *you* a failure? Hardly. It simply makes you incompatible, not a terrible person or a loser.

I am incensed by the term "failed marriage." And I hated it when my mother referred to my first marriage as a "failure." To channel the late Dr. Wayne Dyer, there is no such thing as failure. You can only achieve a result.

The marital adversity you are experiencing now may lead you down an unexpected path to happiness, if you're open and receptive.

Adopting a Success Mindset

Instead of buying into the mentality of divorce as a failure, I invite you to adopt a *success mindset*. What do I mean by that?

Society tells us that we succeed at divorce when we take our spouse to the cleaners. But at what cost? Regardless of who keeps the house, the boat and the 401(k), the emotional cost can be devastating if you carry around your spouse's wrongs long after the ink on the divorce judgment has dried.

Rather than taking your spouse to the cleaners, success is *starting over with a clean slate*. Success is rebuilding your life with a winning attitude: free from grudges, resentments and emotional baggage. The key is not focusing on what you keep but on *what you create* after the divorce is over. Even better, what you start creating *right now*.

I am not suggesting that you walk away from everything. You shouldn't renounce what is rightfully yours. The goal is to release old trappings that do not serve you to make room for the new.

When I divorced, *I chose* to let my ex keep the townhouse. I didn't want the burden of a mortgage, the maintenance expenses or being tied to a location as I was about to start a brand-new profession. So, I drove away in my car, taking with me my computer and my belongings. That's it. That's all

I needed to finish school. I focused on obtaining my degree and building a fresh life and a new career. The first few years were financially challenging, I admit. And my idea of eating out was the dollar menu at Wendy's.

But my life has turned into a downpour of blessings, and I now live happily in a grand country home with a new loving husband of 13 years and three precious dogs.

Are you open to receiving *your blessings*?

Your Marital Breakdown May Be a Blessing in Disguise

Heartache aside, are you willing to consider your marital problems to be a blessing in disguise?

This may be hard to imagine, but marital adversity, like most challenges, presents a golden opportunity to transform your life. You have received an invitation to gain wisdom, laced with an opportunity to do things better, the possibility of creating something greater, and a push to make changes you didn't realize were necessary.

My friend Maya decided to forgive her husband after he had an affair. They are still together, enjoying a stronger, healthier marriage after fending off the crisis.

On the other end of the spectrum, two precious men I know married and divorced the same woman. After their nasty divorces were over, they both thanked her and moved on to happier lives with women who are a better match for them, and they are currently enjoying tremendous prosperity.

While marital discord is painful, envision the possibility that your life can get better whether you keep your spouse or move on. *Either way, you come out a winner.*

Divorce with the End Result in Mind

If you find yourself on the high road to divorce, know that the journey is much smoother if you ride it with the end in mind.

Instead of dreading the divorce process, fearing what will go wrong or hating your spouse and your marriage, focus on creating a future of unlimited possibility. Entertaining negative thoughts about your spouse sends your energy in his or her direction, depleting the resources you need to move forward. The inquiry is not, "How am I going to get through this?" but, "What am I going to do when I get through this?"

And begin doing it! There is no better place to start than where you are, nor a better time than right now—not stuck in the past nor fearing the future, but creating a fresh beginning in this moment, which is all you've got. Contemplate experiences you look forward to and start taking action towards achieving them. You may not get to keep the spouse you originally picked, but you can pick up the pieces of your broken heart and consciously create the happiness you deserve.

Let the healing and creating begin.

Investing in Your Sanity: Getting Help from a Therapist

Your marital situation may be a far cry from what you envisioned when you tied the knot. You may be riding a rollercoaster of crazy emotions you don't even understand, and the people in your life aren't much help. Your pain is real, but only to you...

You don't have to live in pain, and you don't have to go through this ordeal unsupported. A competent mental health professional can help you sort through the issues that lured you into and make you feel unhappy in your marriage. A good therapist can help you understand yourself, make peace with your past and parental damage, and release baggage like trauma and abuse that could be playing in the background.

Therapy can also help you, your spouse and your children prepare to survive the effects of a contentious marriage and/or divorce in which conflict endangers your children's emotional stability and well-being.

With effective therapy, you can overcome feelings of self-doubt or low self-worth and gain a sense of empowerment.

Therapy can help you see clearly after removing blocks that cloud your vision and understanding. Therapy can help you improve your marriage and decide whether to stay married or to move on. Therapy can help you identify those behavior patterns that could repeat themselves in future relationships and lead you to re-enact the same toxic situations you are experiencing with your current partner.

A mental health professional is your first line of defense to preserve your sanity and inner peace. At the very least, a mental health professional can be a sounding board and a source of emotional support.

This is too important to go it alone. So, consider working with a professional to help you cope with the confusing emotions and challenges inherent in an unhappy marriage and/or separation.

First off, let go of any misconceptions that therapists are for crazy people. That is so *passé*! Many people deprive themselves of the support of a therapist, erroneously thinking they do not need it because they are not crazy. What a pity! A shift in attitude could have helped them or their marriages survive. Frankly, I can't fathom navigating all of my life's ups and downs without the support of a neutral party who listens without judgment.

Is therapy right for you? Only you can decide. But I'm here to help you find out for yourself.

Below you'll find some pointers.

Individual or Couples Counseling?

Depending on your situation, you could start with individual therapy to help you work through negative emotions, such as ambivalence, despair, depression and anxiety. Or, if your spouse is amenable, you can start with couples counseling before you "bond" with your therapist.

Your spouse can feel suspicious, intimidated or "ganged up against" by your therapist if you have established a prior relationship.

Couples counseling is useful when the partners cannot resolve conflict on their own, when spouses grow apart and communication breaks down.

It generally centers on assisting the spouses to improve their communication and listening skills, cultivating empathy and applying problem-solving tools to enhance their relationship.

If your marital problems revolve around your sexual relationship, consider couples counseling with a sex therapist. Do your homework and make sure that this practitioner has excellent client reviews and that you and your spouse feel comfortable with the style, gender and approach of the therapist.

Couples counseling is most beneficial early on, before marital woes get out of hand. But most importantly, for counseling to be effective, both parties must be genuinely interested, willing and committed to working things out.

Simply put, dragging your spouse to therapy will not make a difference if he or she does not want to go. It will not work either, if your purpose is to have the therapist confirm that you're right and your partner is wrong, wrong, wrong.

Taking the Edge Off the Divorce Process

How to Choose the Mental Health Professional That Is Right for You

Mental health professionals come in many flavors. They possess different levels of education and experience, have their unique personalities and practice different modalities and techniques. Finding the right therapist will require a little legwork. Here's some useful information to help you make an educated choice.

Typically, therapists have to be licensed and must have post-graduate degrees. They can be Licensed Clinical Social Workers (LCSWs) or possess a Master of Social Work (MSW). And then there are Marriage and Family Therapists (MFTs).

Other options include psychologists, who may have either a Ph.D. (Doctor of Philosophy, with emphasis on psychology) or a Psy.D. (Doctor of Psychology).

None of the above practitioners can prescribe medication for mental health issues like depression and anxiety. So, if you need medication, you must get a prescription from your physician or a psychiatrist, who may have either an M.D. degree (Doctor of Medicine) or a D.O. degree (Doctor of Osteopathic Medicine).

Depending on your location, Psychiatric Mental Health Nurse Practitioners may be authorized to provide therapy *and* prescribe psychiatric medications. This option conveniently allows the client to see only one professional, who will oversee progress, side effects (if any), and dose adjustments.

Is your head spinning yet? Don't be confused by this alphabet soup. The key is to select a practitioner who works well with you. Where to start?

Your insurance plan may cover behavioral treatment and may provide a list of practitioners in your network. This will probably include reputable professionals. I found my favorite therapist on my insurance roster when I was looking for a hypnosis practitioner.

Don't be discouraged if you have no insurance coverage. You may find quality help available at an affordable price. In fact, some of my most competent practitioners were free or came with a low-price tag. Many charitable organizations provide counseling for free or on a sliding scale.

Also, reach out to your local university. Both of the universities I attended offered free counseling by graduate students. I found them to be competent, sensitive and eager to help. Their lack of "real world" experience in no way impaired their effectiveness.

The key is finding a practitioner with whom you have a good rapport. Ask around for referrals—from your friends, doctors, social agencies and clergy. Look for patient reviews online. Verify that this practitioner is conveniently located and has accessible office hours.

Once you have selected a practitioner, pay attention to how you feel speaking to him or her. Do you feel safe sharing your thoughts and feelings? Do you feel supported emotionally, or does it feel too cerebral, too formulaic?

Does this person give you a chance to fully express yourself, or does he or she cut you off? What about body language? Does the therapist make good eye contact with you? Does he or she seem warm and caring—treat you with respect? Is your therapist respectful of your time? Is the therapist paying attention to what you say, or is he or she constantly looking at the clock? Does the couples counselor take control of the sessions and balances the parties' opportunity to talk, or does one party get most of the airtime?

It is critical to feel a connection with your therapist. Give him or her the benefit of a couple of sessions. If there is no rapport, find a different therapist. Trust your gut! Don't be afraid to leave! You may have to retell the same painful story to someone else, but it sure beats being stuck with a therapist who does not meet your needs.

And beware of therapists who jump to conclusions and diagnoses too quickly, and/or tell you to "get out" early in therapy, unless your safety or your children's is at risk. A good therapist would not tell you what to do but would respect your autonomy and guide you to make your own decisions.

If You're in an Abusive Relationship

Proceed with care. Many domestic violence organizations discourage people from seeking couples counseling because it could do more harm than good.

During sessions, the abusive spouse will attempt to dominate the conversation, pretend to be "the nice one," push your buttons and try to upset you, making you likely to react and present yourself as the crazy one in the relationship. You need a therapist who understands the power dynamics and imbalances and won't be bamboozled by the con artist tactics and manipulative behaviors of the abuser.

A competent professional would see right through this. I was lucky that my 5-foot-tall therapist stood up to my big ex-husband and threw him out of counseling. But, unfortunately, manipulative behaviors can sometimes go unnoticed. Play it safe and seek individual therapy first and let your practitioner determine if couples counseling is appropriate in your particular situation.

If You Have Suicidal Thoughts

If you are experiencing severe depression or entertaining suicidal thoughts, get help *immediately.* Contact a suicide hotline in your area and reach out to loved ones who can provide you with the support you need.

You can get through all this. Hang in there. And never hesitate to seek help.

Awakening the Sage within and Making Decisions with Confidence

Before we continue, I'd like to offer you a pep talk about making decisions with confidence.

The problems you are experiencing in your marriage may push you to make major changes in your life and will require you to make critical decisions. Some of them will affect, not only your current situation, but will have ripple effects into your future. Finding yourself at these crossroads may feel overwhelming and intimidating, and you may be afraid of making mistakes.

Do not allow indecision to stop you from claiming the joyous life that is your right. Likewise, do not be paralyzed by fear of making a wrong choice. Making mistakes is an inevitable part of life; and learning from (and correcting) our mistakes is the path to personal growth.

You can do this!

The key to making sound decisions is doing your homework and carefully investigating and weighing your options. And, equally, if not more important, is *making decisions from your highest self.*

What do I mean by that?

Effective solutions can only come to a mind that is free from destructive thought patterns. You should never make major decisions in haste or under the influence of negative emotions, like anger, hatred, victimhood, or motivated by revenge.

Thus, cultivating a peaceful mind is the mechanism for activating your inner sage, releasing your inner wisdom and taking right actions.

Cultivate a Peaceful Mind through Meditation

Meditation is the best way to quiet the mind. Meditation is a highly effective tool to heighten awareness and restore a sense of serenity and inner peace.

The word meditation conjures up all kinds of images, but you do not have to stand up on your head chanting mantras nor lay on a bed of nails. It does not require you to embrace beliefs that conflict with your own. These mysterious associations may scare some people, but they shouldn't frighten you.

Meditation is essentially quieting the mind. Turning off the inner chatter that torments us with thoughts of the past and fear of the future. These ceaseless thoughts steal our attention from living in the present moment, where the action is. Where things happen. Where ideas flow. Where change takes place.

Most of us have so much clutter revolving in our heads we are convinced we cannot turn off our minds. Especially when we obsess about unhappy situations that consume our attention.

Yet, meditation is not about instantaneously drawing a blank for hours at a time. You start by slowing down your thoughts until you eventually feel the bliss of serenity. And once you experience that peace, you will be hooked. You will never get enough of it.

The easiest method of meditation is to sit comfortably with your back straight, close your eyes and follow your breath. Focus your attention on your in-breaths and out-breaths for five to 10 minutes. If thoughts arise while you're meditating, release them and return your attention to your breath. That's it! In time, you can increase the duration of your meditation sessions or try more sophisticated techniques.

As you can see, meditation is simple, free, needs no fancy equipment and you can practice it anywhere at any time. There are countless styles of meditation. Choose one that's right for you. Experiment with different techniques until you discover the one that hits the spot.

You may switch styles at different times, depending on your mood and circumstances. Feel free to play on your own and create a routine that will make you feel refreshed, alert and alive.

Take a class or go on retreat and meet fellow meditators who can support you on your practice. Pick up a book or browse online. The Internet is full of resources, including guided meditation videos to help you get started. Check out Smiling Mind, a free meditation app to get you meditating in five minutes!

One of my favorite spiritual teachers, Tara Brach, has fantastic information on her website, including guided meditations and comprehensive meditation FAQs. Her peaceful demeanor and soothing voice will have you in the zone in no time.

Brach's beautiful teachings have been instrumental in my spiritual evolution, and can support you, too, as you transition from a rocky marriage to an awakened life.

Like many people, you may be skeptical that you can meditate. Anyone can meditate, including you. And once your mind is quiet, you can let your intuition do its job and guide your decisions and actions in every situation.

What Is Intuition?

As you stand bewildered on a fork in the road wondering what to do, realize that you have an internal guidance system that knows the solution to every problem and the answer to every question. It's called intuition. Intuition is your inner sage. It is often referred to as the sixth sense or the "still small voice" within. Intuition is that hunch that nudges you to turn right when you know you're supposed to turn left, only to avoid an accident or a traffic jam.

Intuition directs you to call a friend, and you
out this person was in danger or need, and your cal.
sent. Perhaps it convinced you to walk into an unfai
where you found an elusive item you had been long   ..g
for.

Intuition is always active and available to guide you—
anywhere, anytime. And it responds to your requests for help.
It will help you discover the right answer every time—if you let
it. It will show you the way. When you follow your intuition
and surrender to its guidance, things go smoothly and unfold
in perfection.

Perhaps you have not enjoyed the full benefits of
intuition up to now because you were not in tune with its
power. We are conditioned to rely exclusively on our reasoning
minds, and to reach our solutions from the (limited) pool of
knowledge that we have. So we knock ourselves out over-
thinking the solution to our problems when, in reality, we
would do ourselves a favor if we stepped back and allowed
intuition to step in and reveal the answers.

You Have the Gift of Intuition

You may think intuition is a faculty possessed only by psychics
or saints. But everybody has the gift of intuition—whether or
not they realize it. That includes *you*.

Some people may appear to have a keener intuition.
They seem to mysteriously *know* things hidden to the rest of

us. That is because these people have made a habit of listening to it, trusting it and following where it leads.

You can cultivate your intuition and enjoy its benefits, too. Unleashing the magic of intuition is easier than you think. It merely requires you to get out of the way and let it do its job. It is releasing your ego's need to control every outcome and welcoming the possibility that your path will reveal itself at each junction on the road.

Follow these steps to wake up your intuitive powers:

1. Quiet your mind. Meditate for a few minutes and clear your mind of obsessive thoughts and negative emotions. Negative emotions block the flow of intuition.

2. Articulate in your mind the problem you are seeking to solve. To receive the right answer, you need to pose the right question. Ask the question from a place of integrity and make it your intention to attract the best solution for the highest good. End with this affirmation from Florence Scovel Shinn: "*I am always under direct inspiration; I make right decisions quickly.*"

3. Release your query and allow the answers to come to you without forcing them. Sleep on it, as the saying goes. I prefer to do this exercise before going to sleep, and the answer often comes in a dream or a thought that pops up when I wake up in the morning.

4. Listen for the messages. The answers will come to you, but you can only notice them if you are open and receptive. Use active awareness and pay attention!

While it would be convenient if they appeared on a billboard addressed to you personally, your responses can arrive in in a variety of ways, many of them surprising. They can show up in the form of a thought or idea. They can appear as an image—a mental picture—a word or a song. Your answers can be delivered in a call from a friend or a random encounter with a stranger. You can receive a subtle sign or be struck with a major epiphany.

5. Trust your intuition. Intuition is the opposite of the reasoning mind. Often your intuitive hits will defy common sense. We run into problems when we try to second guess our intuition. Or when we become attached to an outcome and are unwilling to consider that there may be a better way. Get rid of the graspingness. Do not fight your intuitive leads and see where they take you.

6. Act on your intuitive hits. If you feel prompted to do something, go for it! Your surprise blessing may be waiting for you, or a wave of favorable unforeseen events may ensue. I am not suggesting you engage in reckless conduct, but if a seemingly harmless idea pops up—what do you have to lose?

At first glance this may seem senseless to you. But questioning your intuition will neutralize its efficacy. If you can't bring yourself to trust the unknown, start with smaller decisions.

As you strengthen your intuitive abilities and begin to honor and follow your leads, you can delegate larger matters until you stop resisting and permit yourself to go with the flow. You will then move through life feeling confident that you're always in the right place at the right time and taking the correct action.

Rely on your intuition to guide you as you end your relationship with your spouse as it exists today. It will advise you whether to leave or to stay. It will reveal to you the actions you need to take to repair your struggling marriage, or it will show you the way to the door.

Your intuition will become your most trusted adviser in every area of your life. Your intuition will guide you step by step to rebuild your life and attain your highest good. Your inner sage will point the way to freedom and fulfillment. Your inner sage will direct you to your ideal home, your next career or job or the training you need to reach your goals. Your intuition will introduce you to new people and will counsel you whom you need to let go. And just as important, it will intervene and nudge you when you're heading the wrong way.

As you continue to activate your intuitive faculties, you will discover that they are always working for you, even without your asking. And you will feel empowered to make decisions with confidence.

PART II

DO YOU STAY MARRIED OR SHOULD YOU HIT THE ROAD?

How Did You Get Yourself in This Mess and How Do You Get Yourself Out?

Uncover the Traps that Got You in the Wrong Relationship

Now that you're aware that you need to be aware and have been primed on the basics of active awareness, let's explore the issues that got you into this mess, so you can get out of it!

Your Parents' Relationship

Whether or not we like our parents, our relationships with them (or lack thereof) and their relationship with each other shape the way we perceive, interpret and act in the world.

I know, you hate to think you're anything like your parents; but let's face it, you probably are. And that's okay. As children, we saw our parents interacting, and from those interactions we developed an idea of what a marriage should look like and how married people are supposed to behave towards each other.

If you grew up watching your parents yelling and throwing dishes at each other, you may have assumed that was normal and married someone just like your mom or dad. Then, as you find yourself recreating this scenario with your spouse, it dawned on you that having dishes thrown at you is totally uncool.

If your parents had a horrible marriage, you may have vowed not to be like them and looked for a mate who was the exact opposite of your parents. So, you married the most unemotional being you came across. Even though your spouse may not throw dishes at you, he or she may be so dispassionate as to leave you feeling lifeless and unloved.

Or perhaps you married someone who mirrored the behaviors of one or both of your parents, hoping that, by re-enacting their roles, you could re-write their script. You hang on to your marriage, hoping it will eventually bring the happily ever after feeling you wish your parents had.

Maybe your parents enjoyed the perfect relationship. So you feel disappointed because your spouse does not live up to the lofty standards you came to expect from observing your parents' wedded bliss.

Whether your parents were lovebirds or poster children of marital hell, the bottom line is that your parents' dynamics may be playing in the background of your own marriage. But you don't have to repeat your parents' destructive patterns and mistakes.

With the practice of active awareness, you can understand how the interactions in your parents' relationship paved your way into this mess, so you can find your way out. You will be able to make sense of your parents' dynamics, your attitudes regarding those dynamics, and understand how they have shaped your relationship with your spouse.

You will be able to discern whether your parents' interactions contributed to your choosing the wrong spouse or influenced you into the wrong interactions with the right spouse—or wrong interactions with the wrong spouse.

You can then assess if realignment is in order and take action. This knowledge can help you determine if your marriage is doomed to fail or give you the freedom to purposely create a marriage in line with *your* personal ideals.

You don't have to throw the baby away with the bathwater. You get to choose the best qualities from your parents' marriage and release those that do not serve you.

Let's dive in.

Reflections
What was your parents' relationship like?
What did you like about it?
What was terrible about it?
What would you change?
In what ways does your spouse
resemble your father? Your mother?
In what ways is he/she different?

*How did your parents' interactions
influence your view of marriage
and romantic relationships?
What aspects of your parents'
marriage are you repeating in yours?
Which are keepers?
Which need to go?*

Societal Views and Ideas about Marriage and Relationships

If you think your parents did you in, brace yourself. Society screwed you up even more. And the worst part is that you may not even realize it. We are constantly fed images of what relationships look like—on TV, the movies, romance novels.

So we go into this venture, till death do us part, with the ideas and expectations of somebody else—the people who want to sell you books, movies and greeting cards. And what about those pesky people who want to sell you expensive jewelry and trick you into believing that all holidays bring diamonds? Spoiler alert: they don't!

How can we possibly know what we are getting ourselves into when we get married with a set of expectations that bear no resemblance to the harsh realities we live day in and day out? No wonder we end up and stay in unhappy marriages.

Does any of this sound familiar?

- I am nothing without a partner.
- I am incomplete unless I am married with children.
- It's better to be in an awful marriage than being alone.
- Jealousy is a sign of love.
- Boys will be boys - it's okay for men to cheat on their wives.
- Men cheat when they don't find what they need at home.
- Children need both parents to survive.

These are some of the main ingredients in a recipe for disaster. While marriage exists within the context of society, outside sources should not dictate the terms of the most important relationship in your life.

You may have entered your marriage with your eyes closed, blindly following the lead of your society's ideals and norms. You may have felt pressured by friends and relatives asking you, "When are you going to get married?" or by a girlfriend demanding a ring because "It's about time."

Perhaps you feel locked into an unhappy marriage and tolerate objectionable behaviors because they are socially acceptable, while wondering if something is wrong with *you*. But it is never too late to discern where your ideas came from and discard the messages that do not serve you.

Once you identify these negative ideas, you can understand how they influenced your choice of a partner and how they are currently molding your relationship with your spouse. These insights will empower you to replace old ideas with new beliefs that promote self-esteem and healthy relationships, or to end a relationship that is too tainted to salvage.

Here are alternative views to consider:

- I have the wisdom to create a blissful marriage based on my values and ideals.
- I am worthy and can live a full and satisfying life with or without a spouse.
- I deserve respect and fidelity.
- Marriage is wonderful, but I can be happy single, too.
- I am perfectly equipped to raise my children.

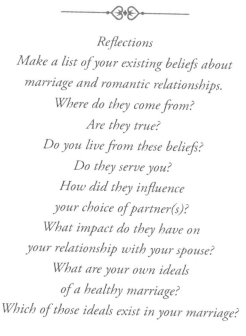

Reflections
Make a list of your existing beliefs about
marriage and romantic relationships.
Where do they come from?
Are they true?
Do you live from these beliefs?
Do they serve you?
How did they influence
your choice of partner(s)?
What impact do they have on
your relationship with your spouse?
What are your own ideals
of a healthy marriage?
Which of those ideals exist in your marriage?

Which are missing and how can you
bring them into your relationship?

Disempowering Beliefs

What we believe about ourselves colors the way we feel, act, relate to others and present ourselves in the world. When we hold negative beliefs about ourselves, we push away the wonderful things we deserve and invite into our lives misery and unhappiness.

These are what I call "disempowering beliefs." Disempowering beliefs are false statements about yourself that you have embraced as truth—so much so that they define who you *think* you are. They disconnect you from who you really are and prevent you from becoming the person you are meant to be. They frequently manifest in our inner chatter as things we tell ourselves, such as, "I am so stupid," or "I can't get anything right," or "I am not good enough." The scripts are many and familiar.

Disempowering beliefs have much in common with the societal views that duped us into awful marriages. They are all around us, come from some of the same places and spill into every area of our lives. They are also the unwanted offerings of our parents, friends and relatives, teachers, church leaders and authority figures.

It is because many of them come from trusted sources that we accept disempowering beliefs as true. We hang on to these beliefs because they are so ingrained that we mistake them for who we really are. Some are blatant, some are subtle—almost imperceptible. These are the most dangerous ones.

As a child, a teacher may have told you that you were stupid or that you wouldn't get far in life. So, now you tell yourself you are a failure and engage in behaviors that make failure inevitable, including in your relationships.

Disempowering beliefs often stem out of unresolved hurts. Unresolved hurts are old hurts that, even though they happened a long time ago, you internalized them, so they continue to have a grip on your life, day in and day out.

Unresolved hurts are like background apps. They run behind the scenes, unperceived, overriding your awareness and blocking the freedom to live a full life. They get triggered by everyday events in unsuspecting ways. Left unchecked, they sneak up on you and can ruin every aspect of your life. These hurts may have constant airtime in your inner chatter, and they probably had an enormous influence on how you selected your partner and why you remain in an unsatisfying relationship.

For example, if one or both of your parents abandoned you as a child, this hurt may have led you to conclude you were worthless and undeserving. Thus, you picked a partner who denigrates you and makes you feel unworthy, and you stay stuck in the relationship because you feel you don't deserve any better. And you live in fear of being abandoned again.

Unless you uncover and deactivate them, unresolved hurts will continue to take over your life.

Some disempowering beliefs result from how we interpret our experiences. Let's say your first love betrayed you. You felt humiliated and reasoned from those actions that you were ugly and undesirable and, from that day forward, decided that no one would love you. So you married the first person who gave you attention and felt lucky that he or she did not realize—at least not yet—that you were wholly unlovable. And you feel stuck in an unsatisfying relationship because you're convinced that no one else could possibly want to be married to you.

Now consider other possibilities... Maybe your flame had issues. Or was emotionally broken and didn't know how to love. But instead, you concocted a story that weakened you, when you could have written a story that empowered you. How about: "Next!" or "I deserve better."

Many disempowering beliefs are self-inflicted. Some result from comparing ourselves to others and concluding we don't measure up to an artificial standard of perfection. This is very common in our society, which worships unattainable standards of beauty, and values certain races, lifestyles and professions at the expense of uniqueness and individuality.

So, you feel "less than" because your boobs aren't big enough, or you don't have a six-pack or earn a six-figure salary. You fill in the blanks. We are tricked into desiring false ideals and pay an outrageous price by shortchanging or hating ourselves.

Unfortunately, either alone or put together, disempowering beliefs paint a picture of ourselves that invalidates us. When we believe these statements and internalize them, they ultimately conceal and replace our identities, and we act from that illusion without even realizing it.

So, we end up living, not our own lives, but the lives that belong to the people we wrongly conclude we are. It's like living every day as Halloween night, wearing a costume rather than showing our true selves. Would you go through life wearing a mask? Yet, that is, in fact, what you do when you allow disempowering beliefs to control you.

Disempowering beliefs act like magnets that draw us to partners who are wrong for us, but the perfect match for the impostor we have mistaken for ourselves. You may have settled for the wrong partner thinking you didn't deserve any better. This is because disempowering beliefs erode self-esteem and steal your power.

Since disempowering beliefs shape your attitudes and behaviors and attract undesirable conditions, it is essential to uncover those beliefs, and replace them with beliefs that support a life that is joyous and abundant.

When you use active awareness to examine these false beliefs, you dissolve their power over you. You pave the way for revealing and cherishing your precious self. You can then realize how you have cheated yourself of the full life that is meant for you. Once you come to this realization, you can discover and delight in a smorgasbord of unlimited possibility.

Unmask the impostor that is living your life and say, "Hasta la vista!" Make a list of every negative belief you hold about yourself. Examine each disempowering belief, uncover its origin, and substitute it with a positive thought that brings out who you really are.

Reflections
Pay attention to your inner chatter.
What do you tell yourself?
What do you believe about yourself?
What beliefs about yourself hold you back?
Make a list of hurtful events you remember from your childhood.
Recall the events in your mind.
(If any events are too painful to process, such as incest or sexual abuse, stop this exercise and seek the assistance of a professional therapist.)
What do these events make you believe about yourself?
Are these beliefs true?
What thoughts could you choose to replace them?
Who would you be if you didn't believe those beliefs?
Would this person be married to your spouse?

Lack of Self-Love

Here comes the hard part. You may have something to do with this, too. You may be with the wrong spouse in part because you do not love yourself. You heard me right. You do not love yourself.

Louise Hay, the legendary self-help luminary, said that, when working with clients, regardless of the problem, there was only one thing she worked on, and that was *loving the self.* According to Hay, loving ourselves works miracles. Not loving ourselves, however, wreaks havoc in every area of our lives, whether it is relationships, finances, even health.

Loving ourselves is not arrogance, selfishness or conceit. It means having a healthy self-image, valuing ourselves and others, and accepting nothing but respect in our personal interactions. When we don't love ourselves, we sell ourselves short, and settle for less than what is rightfully ours.

Feelings of low self-worth broadcast themselves like an enormous billboard, sending a signal to the world that we are undeserving of anything good and feeling grateful to accept the crumbs others throw at us.

In our love lives, they act as self-fulfilling prophesies, attracting into our lives mates that do not value us or treat us well, and keeping us stuck in unhealthy relationships.

Like disempowering beliefs, feelings of self-loathing originate from many sources, internal and external to us, and are equally damaging. Like disempowering beliefs, you can also dissolve them with active awareness.

Learning to love yourself is the first step in turning around your life and your relationships. Loving yourself means honoring your needs while treating everyone with the same respect and consideration you wish for yourself.

Feelings of self-loathing didn't occur overnight and can take some time and practice to dissolve. Loving the self will manifest by taking baby steps in the right direction.

Once you "change the billboard" and send a different message, you will attract different people and situations. Your new and improved confidence will lead to improved dynamics in your existing relationships, attract healthier new relationships, and provide you with the wisdom and courage to ditch relationships that harm you.

In the upcoming chapters we will boost self-love through empowering self-care practices. For now, begin exploring whether you don't love yourself enough, and if feelings of self-loathing tricked you into choosing and staying with the wrong partner.

Learning to love the self is a lifetime pursuit. And an invaluable one at best. For a deep exploration of this subject, I highly recommend Louise Hay's classic bestseller *You Can Heal Your Life*, as well as anything published by this amazing woman. It is full of insights that can help you transform every area of your life. It is available in DVD and audiobook format, too, and it is a must-have in your collection of personal growth resources.

Reflections
Do you love yourself?
Do you put others (including your spouse)
first, to your own detriment?
Do you feel you don't deserve better than
what you get in your relationships?

*Do you tolerate from others behaviors
you wouldn't inflict on them?
Do you accept less than what you think is fair? Why?
Look around - who are your friends and associates?
Do you surround yourself with people who love you? Cheat you?
Belittle you? Encourage you?*

You Didn't See It Coming: Missing the Red Flags

As your dream love morphed into your worst nightmare, you may wonder... "How did this happen? Why didn't I see this coming?" In hindsight, we're all 20-20, but moving forward requires us to look back, so we can learn from our mistakes and make better choices in the future. You are probably asking yourself, "Were the signs there? How could I have missed them? Or did I ignore them? Why?"

This investigation is an excellent starting point, and the results may surprise you. Let's take a look.

The Grand Prize We Create after God's Image and Likeness

It is no secret that, when we fall in love, we tend to see our partners through a special lens: the lens showing them in the best light. The way in which we *want* to see them. As God's gift to us.

Maybe you attributed to this person qualities that weren't there. Think about it… Has a love-struck friend ever asked you to meet "The One," and the encounter left you wondering what the fuss was all about?

Well, we all do the same thing. You probably attributed to your spouse qualities that you wished he or she had. And just like you didn't have the nerve to tell your friend to run for the nearest exit, your friends didn't tell you because they didn't want to hurt your feelings. After all, if you didn't heed their advice and married this person, your friendship might have been over.

Here's a test. Have you ever broken up with someone and found out afterwards that your friends despised him or her?

It happened to me. I was dumped by a guy I didn't even like, only to find out my friends were thrilled to see him out of my life (and theirs). I had no idea that my friends loathed this successful, mild-mannered guy my mom would have totally approved. I missed the particular flaws my friends disdained—I disliked him for other reasons. Imagine how we fail to notice the defects of someone we *do* like!

Does this ring a bell? Bring up the subject of old flames next time you get together with your buddies and brace yourself for a surprise. And when you get home, pull out your journal, unload your mental notes, and reflect on how you allowed your judgment to be impaired in past relationships. Those insights may apply to your current situation.

Ignoring the Red Flags

Possibly, your spouse displayed early in your relationship the very behaviors that are leading you to consider divorce, but you didn't see them, misunderstood their significance, justified them or downplayed their importance. The signs were always there, but you didn't pick them up.

Perhaps you saw the red flags, but you ignored them. If so, you need to ask yourself why. Maybe they were rare and isolated incidents you attributed to stress or other factors. Moments in which your partner lost self-control over an otherwise carefully staged persona. Maybe those little pink flags turned red over time, and those behaviors escalated from the slightly unpleasant into the intolerable.

It is essential that you look back on this, not to berate yourself or to make yourself feel stupid. Why you missed these red flags is critical.

If you're lucky, your friends will remind you, at the end of the saga, of all of those insufferable qualities that you hate about your spouse that you blew off until it was too late. *And pay attention.* These are the mental notes you must scrutinize to ensure you don't fall into the same trap again, should you divorce and feel tempted to hook up with his or her clone.

Reflections

*Did your spouse turn out to be a different
person from whom you thought he or she was?
What has changed? Your spouse or your
perception of him or her?
Did your spouse fall short or turned out to be
different from what you expected?
What behaviors do you find offensive?
When did you start noticing them?
Looking back, can you recall earlier instances
when your spouse engaged in the same
behaviors, but you didn't notice?
Why didn't you notice?
Did you notice but dismissed them?
Downplayed them? Misinterpreted them?
Justified them? Why?
Have your friends ever said anything about
those behaviors before or after you got married?
How did you react? By dismissing them?
Excusing them?*

Can You Love Your Spouse "As Is"?

Sorting Through Unrealistic Expectations

Your spouse deserves to be loved, just like you do, with all imperfections. Perhaps by someone else—not necessarily you. That's why it's imperative to look at this objectively and with an open mind.

Whether societal, self-inflicted or family-based, unrealistic expectations are a huge reason men and women enter marriages that turn hideously disappointing. Marriage takes work, no matter how wonderful the parties are. When you factor in unrealistic expectations, the relationship will falter the moment reality sets in.

The Wedding Fantasy

In our society, the fantasy wedding has replaced the authentic joy of tying the knot with the love of your life. The wedding industry has convinced us that a fairytale wedding with expensive dresses, lavish receptions and exotic honeymoons is the yellow brick road to happily ever after.

In fact, no self-respecting wedding would be complete without a photo booth and a food truck for the munchies that inevitably follow cocktail hour, a four-course dinner and a fully loaded sundae bar. We buy into a fictitious model packed with unnecessary trimmings designed to make us look and feel like a celebrity.

It's okay to bask in the joy of wedding planning. And there is no harm delighting in being the center of attention—if only for a day.

However, in the dark world of Bridezillas, things can get so out of control that the meaning of marriage gets lost in the hoopla. Remember Carrie in the first *Sex and the City* movie?

Fast forward a few years, or just months, and many couples recognize that they were more excited about the wedding than about the hardcore realities of married life. Chores like paying bills, cooking dinner and taking out the garbage dominate the marital landscape, to the horror of many newlyweds.

And suddenly, Prince Charming looks plain without his Christian Dior tuxedo and the Princess appears unglamorous with unshaven legs. So, it comes as no surprise that many couples head to divorce court before the main event has been paid for. The "luckier ones" wake up from their slumber late enough to have paid for their weddings and accumulated enough material trappings to fight over in a bitter divorce.

Were You in Love with Your Partner or with Something External?

Even the most naïve among us knows that marriage will come with good times and bad times. It's stated plainly in traditional wedding vows. The inevitable ups and downs of marriage can be better weathered when you go through them with someone you love. But what happens when it was not this human being you were actually in love with?

When you marry someone for any reason not intrinsic to him or her—whether it's looks, money, status, a fancy car—you risk your marriage will collapse when any of these external factors comes off the table.

A change in circumstances can make the person you married seem much less desirable and sticking it out a lot more painful. So, people who married out of interest in external traits have an uphill battle keeping their marriages alive—or staying alive in their marriages. Unless they can find other endearing qualities that make their partners "keepers," such a union is bound to fail.

Someone I know married her boss while still having feelings for the love of her life. Why? Because her boss drove a Porsche! I don't need to tell you that the love of her life is living happily ever after with the love of *his* life while her marriage crashed.

In our society, looks, power, money and prestige have become aphrodisiacs that make partners desirable in our eyes, because we assume they will provide the things that are supposed to make us happy. While money does buy nice things, a woman who marries a man for his money will earn every penny. And men who marry a woman solely for her beauty will be in for a shock when her breasts go south. Being married to someone you love is hard enough, and no money in the world can buy you the joy of sharing your life with someone you treasure and treasures you back.

Reflections
What attracted you to your spouse?
What were your reasons for marrying?
Do these qualities hold true to this day?
If not, are you willing to love your spouse for who he or she is? In other words, does your spouse have other qualities that make him or her a worthy partner in your eyes?
Examine your own value system. Are there any other qualities that you value that influenced your choice of a partner?

Did You Marry a Project?

Everybody loves a good challenge, and sometimes our other halves have a little room for improvement. After all, marriage is about teaming up with someone who brings out the best in us.

Minor cosmetic changes are okay, but things get dicey when we marry intending to change our partners into someone they are not—or have no desire to be.

If you dismissed your partner's worst defects intending to eliminate them after marriage, you have set yourself up for a life of resentment and bitter disappointment. While it is commendable to encourage and support your spouse to reach his or her highest potential, core issues like ambition, drive and values are set. Your spouse will resist your pushiness and resent you for it. And you will hate your spouse for not living up to your unrealistic expectations.

Reflections
What characteristics of your
spouse would you change?
Were these characteristics there,
before you married?
Did your spouse ever express any desire to
improve in these areas?
Or did you assume your spouse would
change—or that you could change him or
her—after the wedding?

Surprise! You Married a Con Artist

Perhaps you didn't see the red flags because there weren't any. The person you married turned out to be different from the one you dated. After much soul searching, you may conclude that your spouse *lied* to you. You did your due diligence and entered your marriage in good faith. Maybe your partner portrayed a charismatic persona until you fell under a spell and revealed a completely different "real self" the moment you said, "I do."

This is very common in abusive relationships. The classic abuser is charming, affectionate, considerate—the ultimate impostor. The perfect catch to the outside world. But once you are trapped under the spell, the con artist will use every trick in the bag to keep you trapped.

An abusive partner will try to destroy your self-esteem and make you question your sanity with constant insults and put downs and alienate you from your support systems.

I know this well. It happened to me. Before we married, my ex-husband was insanely attentive. He showered me with presents and brought me flowers every time we met. It was flattering to be placed on this sky-high pedestal, only to have it knocked down less than 24 hours after our wedding. He said unequivocally, on our way to our honeymoon, that from then on everything would be different; everything would change. I cried all the way to Mexico and wondered how I could have made such a terrible mistake. How I would undo it was an even more terrifying question, one that took me years to sort out.

Trust is an integral part of any human relationship. If your spouse conned you into marriage or turned out to be abusive after you tied the knot—do not second guess yourself. And do not beat yourself up because you didn't see it coming.

Get help—fast! A quality mental health professional is your best line of defense. Get a recommendation from a trusted friend, your doctor or a social services agency.

In the sections that follow, I will share with you empowering techniques to keep you strong and centered while ending a toxic relationship and ways of staying sane in a relationship you are not yet ready to leave.

Are You in an Abusive Relationship?

As you look at this heading, you may think, "This doesn't apply to me." Think again. You may be in an abusive relationship and not even know it. This is particularly true for men, who may believe only women can be victims of domestic abuse. Read this section anyway. It may be eye-opening and could literally save you or someone you know.

If your partner physically hurts you, you are definitely in an abusive relationship, and your safety (and your children's) should be your first priority.

Nothing justifies being hurt by your partner. *Get help, plan a safe exit and get out!* In this chapter, you will find resources to support you in your flight to freedom.

If your spouse doesn't hit you, or does so when "drunk, or high, or stressed out," you may think you are not in an abusive relationship. Perhaps you sense that something is not right in your marriage, and you wonder if you are indeed in an abusive relationship. You may dismiss your suspicions as vain imaginings. After all, your partner can be so loving at times…

There are so many nuances to domestic abuse and so many misconceptions, that both men and women are trapped in abusive relationships without realizing it. Just because you aren't bouncing off the walls or aren't covered in bruises does not mean you are not in an abusive relationship.

Perhaps you don't fit the picture of the abuse victim you hold in your mind. You may think domestic abuse is something that happens to women, the poor, minorities, the uneducated, the weak—in other words, *not you*. But in reality, domestic abuse does not know or respect labels of any kind.

Domestic abuse is about power and control. Domestic abuse can be as subtle as innuendo and as far-reaching as Hollywood stars. No wonder women and men are confused about this hot topic, which touches the lives of many people we know and love—even in our own families.

In an interview with Anderson Cooper, Jennie Willoughby, the ex-wife of Rob Porter, ousted White House Staff Secretary, stated that she didn't realize she was in an abusive relationship. People wondered how that was possible. After all, she is a beautiful, intelligent, articulate woman, and her husband was a handsome, charming, successful man.

Adding insult to injury, people often told Willoughby how lucky she was to be married to him. Because a man like Porter did not fit our society's stereotype of "the wife beater," Willoughby and people in her world did not initially recognize the signs.

Emotional abuse is covert, yet just as dangerous—if not more—than physical abuse. Unlike physical injuries, emotional wounds can go undetected and, without intervention, they can lead to lasting damage.

The emotional abuser will destroy you—not your body—but your soul, your self-worth and the core of your being. In the absence of physical injuries, you may not recognize the signs and fail to seek help. People who care for you and would otherwise help you may also be in the dark and leave you unsupported, thinking you're married to the catch of the century.

My friend Laura puts it well: "*You get sucked in and don't realize it until you get out, and when you step back and look at it, it's eye-opening and awakening. You realize you were minimized. But it doesn't matter why, whether it's alcohol or mental health issues.*"

That's why it is so important to identify the signs. Consider this non-technical test: does your partner treat you in ways that make you feel bad about yourself?

You will find here tools to help you recognize whether you're in an abusive relationship, and resources to help you break free from abuse.

Ending and surviving domestic abuse is a complex issue that deserves full exploration, which I will do in an upcoming book. For now, answer the questions listed below, and discover for yourself if you are living with an abuser, so you can reclaim your power, survive and thrive.

You Are in an Abusive Relationship if Your Partner:

- Insults you, criticizes you and puts you down.
- Calls you names.
- Acts jealously and falsely accuses you of promiscuous behaviors.
- Isolates you from your support systems - prevents you or discourages you from seeing and talking to family and friends.
- Attempts to control what you do, where you go and whom you see.
- Controls your access to money and interferes with your ability to earn and spend money.
- Interferes with your ability to work or get an education.
- Threatens to harm you or intimidates you with frightening looks, words and actions.
- Goes on angry fits and destroys property in your presence.
- Harms your children and pets.
- Intimidates you with weapons or objects that could cause physical harm.
- Tells you you're crazy or tries to make you think you're crazy.
- Forces you to have sexual relations or engage in sexual acts you do not want to take part in.

Safety First

Are you living with an abuser? Domestic abuse is not a situation that resolves itself and will escalate over time. If your spouse is abusive, *get help*. Talk to a trusted mental health professional. Reach out to an organization in your community that provides domestic violence assistance. A counselor can help you confirm if you're in an abusive relationship and provide you with the emotional guidance you need to boost your self-esteem, heal your wounds and rebuild your life.

If you're in a dangerous situation, they can help you get out safely and sanely. These organizations are familiar with your legal system, and can help you understand, protect, and exercise your rights. They can offer you ideas on how to preserve evidence to support your case, including taking pictures of damage inflicted on you and your property and keeping a journal documenting incidents of abuse.

Some offer a variety of safety nets for women and their children, like shelter, access to financial support and empowerment training. They can direct you to available educational and employment opportunities in your area, so you get back on your feet as you escape from your destructive relationship.

Domestic abuse is disempowering; but remember that you are perfectly equipped to thrive in life. And you are not alone. Many people successfully end destructive relationships. You can, too.

Abusers don't change—get help, plan a safe escape and get out!

In the United States, contact the National Domestic Violence Hotline for resources and information. If you don't live in the United States, look in the Resources page at the end of this book for domestic violence organizations in your country.

Besides working with your local domestic abuse organization, strengthen your support systems, and do the empowering exercises in the following chapters to preserve your sanity as you make your way to freedom and fulfillment.

Do You Really Want Out?

Life on the Fence

I know what you're thinking… You're wondering, "Do I really want out? Is it really that bad? Would I even be better off if I leave? Things could get better, right?"

These are legitimate questions you need to ask yourself, but most importantly, to answer honestly after careful consideration.

Leaving the one you chose for better or for worse till death do us part is never easy. It is the death of the fondest dreams you held at one time. This is the person you loved. Your pick for a mate, for life. You may still hang on to the illusion of a joyful life together.

Feelings of ambivalence will take you in every direction—and that's good. Because you need to explore these issues from various perspectives. Then, and only then, can you make an informed decision to leave or to stay.

In the sections that follow, we will do some soul-searching exercises to assist you in examining your personal situation, to help you decide the best course for you—at this time. Remember, relationships are living beings and things can change quickly. Keep these exercises handy and revisit them when feelings of doubt and ambivalence creep up again.

Is It Really That Bad?

Here come the hard questions. How bad is it—really? Are you having a bad day, a bad year—a bad life? After a big blow-up, you may feel like it's over and there's no way back. Or perhaps it is those petty things that accumulate day in and day out that lead you to the inescapable conclusion that your spouse will never be the partner you deserve.

A big blow-up may give you the resolve to end your marriage, but it doesn't necessarily present the best circumstances to make a graceful exit. Ending a marriage is not a decision you should make impulsively or while under the influence of anger.

Take Relationship Inventory

Make a list of what's important to you in a marriage. The must-haves. The nice-to-haves. The dealbreakers. This will come in handy if you contemplate reconciliation. It will give you clarity to renegotiate the terms of your marriage going forward and set the tone for an improved, respectful relationship.

Dissect the Pros and Cons

No marriage is 100 percent good or 100 percent bad. Like everything else in life, your marriage probably has good things and bad things. And those good things are what keep you in. The question is, does the good outweigh the bad? Are the good things significant enough that they overshadow the bad stuff? Do they make it more palatable? Or are you staying in for other reasons unrelated to the quality of your relationship?

This is important stuff, so take out your journal and write it all out. Let it flow as a stream of consciousness and write everything that comes to mind.

What's Good about Your Marriage?

Right now you may think your spouse is the devil incarnate but take an honest look. He or she must do some things right, no? Maybe your spouse is an excellent parent, a terrific cook, is a wonderful friend and you have fun together, even if not often enough. Maybe your partner is hardworking and honest. Or perhaps you're married to a horrible human being with few, if any, redeeming qualities.

What's important here is making a heartfelt effort to see good in this person and in your relationship, regardless of your differences. And write it down.

What's Bad?

The bad things can be all those things that annoy us, from the little pet peeves to the biggies. They can range from leaving clothes on the floor, to forgetting anniversaries, inability to hold a job—you name it. Keep going and don't hold back. How pervasive are these behaviors?

What's Intolerable?

Some behaviors are total dealbreakers, particularly abusive behaviors, whether physical or emotional. No one should stay in a relationship in which they don't feel safe or in which they are oppressed, unable to fully express who they are meant to be. Abuse to family members, friends and pets are also dealbreakers.

Any behaviors that endanger you, whether done recklessly or intentionally, are serious red flags you should never overlook. Pay attention.

You must have your own list of intolerables. What is unacceptable to you?

Reasons to Leave

Now this is different from what's bad about the marriage. Some seemingly minor issues can turn major when put in their proper perspective. Those paltry things your spouse does that bother you can reflect a more serious problem in his or her character or in your relationship.

Look for those behavior patterns that reveal these underlying problems. My friend Jean's case is a classic. For at least 12 months, she repeatedly asked her husband to hang some pictures in the kitchen. And he didn't. One day she looked at the pictures leaning against the wall and decided that she had enough. It was over. When she dropped the "D Bomb," he offered to hang the darn pictures. But it was too late. The unhung pictures were a testament to her husband's lack of regard for her needs, which manifested in other ways in their relationship. Clearly, her decision to leave was not about the pictures.

Ask yourself: "What is it really about? Why are you *really* considering exiting your marriage?"

Reasons to Stay

Marriage has its benefits. These benefits can make it more desirable to stay together than splitting up.

Why are you still married? Maybe there's synergy in your relationship that would be lost if you went in separate ways. Perhaps your spouse brings to your life a quality you treasure and are unlikely to find with someone else.

You may have perfectly valid reasons to stay in your marriage. The question is, are they enough? Let's dig in deeper.

You Still Love Your Partner

This is the most compelling reason to stay married. After all, you married this person because you were in love and wanted to spend the rest of your lives together. Even though things are not perfect, you stick around wishing for the best. You hope to rekindle the fire and resurrect the love and devotion you once shared.

Many couples can work things out and stay together, perhaps even stronger after fending off the crisis of imminent separation. It is possible. It can happen to you. But it takes work and commitment from both of you. Are you up to it? How about your spouse? We will explore this in a following section.

Reflections
Do you still love your spouse or
are you just like a pair of old shoes?
Do you love your spouse as much as
you did when you first married?
Has the love cooled off?
Can you heat things up?
Make a list of the things that brought you together.
Are they still there?
What is necessary for you to be happy in your relationship?
What adjustments do you need your spouse to make?
What adjustments do you need to make?

Your Spouse Is Not 100 Percent Bad

Your spouse drives you crazy and can be mean at times. You feel like killing him or her—often. But your partner *can* be loving, tender, generous, funny, charming, witty. The list can go on and on.

Here are key questions to consider: Is that just potentiality? Is that enough? Are you just getting a taste of the good stuff? Or is it the main course? Do you feel like you're served a 3-shrimp cocktail followed by a huge mound of box mashed potatoes? Or the box mashed potatoes followed by an exquisite sliver of chocolate cake, after you're already stuffed?

Your spouse has unlimited potential to be and do amazing things. But does he or she *choose* to live up to that potentiality, or just teases you with "what could be"—most likely when it's convenient?

Balance is key to any relationship, and the good qualities should be enough to neutralize the less desirable ones. A decision to stay should not be based exclusively on pleasant behaviors exhibited on special occasions, and which are not at the core of your partner's personality. You must do the math to make an informed decision to continue your relationship or to call it quits.

Reflections
What qualities do you treasure
in your spouse? Which do you hate?

*What percentage of the time
is your spouse mean? Nice?
What are the core behaviors?
Are your needs satisfied by the number of good
things and qualities your spouse brings to the
table, or do you feel hungry for more?*

Does the Good Outweigh the Bad–Proportionally?

For this reflection, I am going to borrow from the legal world. In reaching decisions, judges look at the "totality of the circumstances" and engage in "balancing tests." It is essential to look at the full picture and balance the equities.

When you weigh the good things against the bad things, they must be in balance, or tip in favor of the good. But to make a proper judgment, you must assign a value to each of these items and give them their proper weight.

For example, if your spouse's greatest defects are in areas that are not that important, like keeping a messy sock drawer, is it worth ending your marriage over sock discombobulation?

On the other hand, does your spouse abuse you or the children? Fail to provide financial or emotional support? You have your own set of deliverables, and only you can decide when enough is enough.

As I stated earlier, ask yourself if there is a pattern or underlying theme to the offensive behaviors. For example, do your partner's actions show a lack of consideration, respect or love? Or is he or she generally careless? Or simply absent minded? Can these defects be fixed with sincere effort? Can you make changes to the way you interact that would neutralize these differences?

Most importantly, how significant are these issues to your quality of life?

How Are These Issues Likely to Play Out in the Future? Get Better? Get Worse? Become More or Less Important?

Let's face it. It is no secret that our worst character traits get magnified as we get older. So, those petty annoyances will probably compound into major disturbances. If you are bothered by your partner's forgetfulness, how are you going to feel when senility kicks in? Can you handle it?

Is the fact that you're married to a homebody who hates going to bars likely to bother you as much when you turn 40 in a few years? Or will you lose your mind when you find yourselves retired with nothing in common 10 or 20 years from now?

Ask yourself if it is worth ending a relationship now over issues that will be moot in the not-so-distant future. Or is it time to run for the door while you still can?

Regret is no place to be. If the clock is ticking and you want to have children, but you suspect your spouse will not be a good parent, end the relationship before age and infertility become a barrier to your dreams.

That applies to other important aspirations for which time is of the essence. You have work to do—do it now!

Would You Be Happier Alone?

I said it before, and I will say it again: you deserve to be happy. So does your spouse. Happiness is a serious business. You are not doing yourself—or your partner—any favors by staying in a relationship that makes you miserably unhappy.

If, after doing all the exercises, you feel convinced that you will never be happy together, you both deserve a second chance to start a fresh life apart that can bring you the joy missing from your life now.

Reflections
What are your partner's strengths and weaknesses?
What attracted you to him or her? Is it still there?
Do the good qualities outweigh the bad?
What aspects of the marriage work well?
What's not working in your marriage?
Can it be fixed?
What's intolerable?
Do you feel safe?
Would you be happier with your partner or alone?

Have You Given It Your Best?

If You Divorce Now–Will You Regret It Later?

While drowning in the misery of my marriage, I came across a frightening statistic: 50% of people who divorced regretted their decision and wished they had worked harder at saving their marriages. Not being a natural quitter, I wondered if I would end up in that 50% regret percentile. Would I feel guilty, down the line, that I bailed out too soon? That I didn't try hard enough? Regret is an ugly destination, and most of the time there is no way back.

That was many moons ago, and regret statistics are hard to come by. But more recent studies confirm that, indeed, between 32% and 50% of divorced people *do regret* having made the move. These people wish they had worked harder at their relationships and stayed married. The exact percentages depend on who did the studies.

The Daily Mail, a British newspaper, reported in 2014 that a survey of 2000 divorced men and women conducted in the UK indicated that 50% of respondents regretted their decision to divorce. On the other hand, a 2016 relationship study conducted by Avvo, an online legal services marketplace, showed that 68% of respondents (and a whopping 73% of female respondents) did not regret getting divorced.

But regardless of whose statistics you prefer to believe, my point remains the same. Regret is a distinct possibility you must carefully consider if you desire to move forward in true freedom. Unless you find yourself in an abusive relationship (in which case, *get help, plan a safe escape and get out!*) it is a good idea to give your relationship a *reasonable* opportunity.

You don't want to be in the 32% or 50% of people wishing they were still together with their ex-spouses. All I'm saying is to give it an honest, *reasonable* chance, not to die trying.

In my case, I made the wise choice to find out. We did have a period of peace, but it was short-lived and clearly unsustainable. Although it took me years to figure things out and conclude, beyond a reasonable doubt, that leaving my husband was the right thing to do, I feel satisfied that I gave it a fair chance and made the correct decision. No regrets.

I sincerely hope that you get to that same place.

Let's analyze some important considerations.

Is It Worth Giving It Another Chance?

Take an honest look at the state of your relationship. Is it in trouble or irreparably broken? Has too much damage and hurt been done? Have you grown too far apart to meet somewhere in between? Is the glue that brought you together not there anymore? Is there another brand of glue that could keep you together?

Are You Willing to Give It Another Chance or Are You Drained?

Be honest with yourself. Turning around a troubled relationship requires tremendous effort and energy. Going through the motions in a symbolic gesture is an exercise in futility. Take time out to gauge your energy levels.

Are you too tired to try? If you are, consider a temporary separation to think it through and recharge your batteries. The exercises ahead will help you power up for the journey in or out of your relationship.

Does Your Spouse Want to Work Things Out?

It takes *two* to make a marriage work. There's no point in knocking yourself out if your partner doesn't value the relationship.

Is he or she sincere about working things out? Or is your spouse putting on an act to pacify you and keep you in the trap? Is your spouse offering cosmetic changes with no change in substance? Talk is cheap, and actions speak louder than words.

Ruminate about this: Is your spouse capable of working things out? Really...

The road to hell is paved with good intentions, so meaning well *by itself* is not good enough. Your spouse needs to prove his or her commitment and demonstrate the ability to team up with you to resurrect your marriage.

Take an Honest Look at Yourself: Do You Contribute to Marital Strife?

Just as your spouse does annoying things to you, you may annoy him or her, too, and not even know it. My friend Lucy, a divorce lawyer, pointed out that, when clients listed their complaints about their soon-to-be-exes, she thought to herself, "*I* do that."

Are you willing to look within and recognize the things you do that may cause problems in your relationship? Are you amenable to finding ways you can relate better to your mate?

The 2016 study conducted by Avvo I cited earlier also found that 64% of women surveyed said their husbands were fully responsible for the breakdown of their marriages as compared to only 44% of the men. Only 29% of the women respondents, as opposed to 42% of the men, thought that both spouses shared the blame.

A marriage is a party of two. Step out of blame into responsibility and grab the bull by the horns. The point of the reflections is not to demonize your partner, but to understand why you are in this mess so you can get out of it.

Reflections
Pay attention to your
interactions with your spouse.
Do you engage in annoying
behaviors? On purpose?
What do you do when your partner does
something that displeases you?
Do you react? Respond?
Is there a better option?
Are you willing to try it?
What happens when you do?
Practice active awareness and be the observer.
Pause before you act.
Catch yourself when things aren't going
smoothly and choose again.

What Keeps You In?

Traps that Keep You in the Relationship

You're looking out the window with your sneakers on, pondering whether to stay or to run as fast as you can. But you're still in. Why? There's no escaping until you figure out what are the barriers to your freedom. Unless you identify them, you won't be able to overcome them.

And sometimes that's not enough. It happened to me. I felt trapped in a miserable situation for lack of support systems and an exit strategy. So it took years of strengthening myself, so I could get out on my terms and feel confident enough to start over. And that's what I hope this book will help you to achieve, should you decide to go that route.

We will look at the common traps. I'm sure you have a list of your own. Stare them in the face and, with active awareness and relentless practice, deactivate them, one by one, until they lose their grip on you.

While powerful, these obstacles are not insurmountable, and you can overcome them if leaving your relationship is best for you.

The key is to explore each of the reasons that keep you in, clear your head, and make your decision to leave or to stay from a place of strength and power, not fear and weakness.

Poor Self-Esteem

We already identified poor self-esteem as one of the causes that lured you into this unfortunate relationship in the first place. If you entered into your marriage with poor self-esteem, marital problems are likely to erode it even further.

Unhealthy self-esteem will snatch your power to stand up for yourself and claim the satisfying life that is your birthright. You need to spot those thoughts that tell you that what you currently have is as good as it gets. That you don't deserve any better. Listen to those voices and learn to quiet them down.

You have no project but yourself! You need to rebuild your confidence and become best friends with the amazing person living inside of you.

It takes time and practice, but you are perfectly equipped to be the best you possible! Otherwise, you wouldn't be here. That is your sacred mission, and you have within you all the ingredients to make it happen. This book will provide you with strategies to support you on your empowerment journey.

You need to convince yourself that being your best self is the ultimate gift you can bring to this world.

Reflections
Do you believe you don't deserve a relationship
that is better than the one you're currently in?
Is having a spouse, albeit one that doesn't make
you happy, better than having no spouse at all?
Do you think no one better than your current
partner could possibly love you?
Do you fear you can't make it
in the world on your own?

Lack of Support Systems

Feeling unsupported is a powerful reason to stay with a person who makes your life hell. Getting out of an unhappy marriage can be an overwhelming proposition under the best of circumstances, let alone without a pep team. If your family or community frowns upon divorce, you will lack the support to make—and carry out—the decision to end your marriage and start over.

Perhaps they do not know what's happening to you and, therefore, haven't been there for you. And if you're married to a con artist who is portraying an unfavorable picture of you,

you may look like the bad guy with the people who would stand up for you, so it seems like *you* are the problem.

Whatever the case, you need to put together your support team—soon. This is too important to go it alone. The good news is that there's lots of help available, waiting for you to reach out and grab it.

Even if your family and friends won't support your decision to end your marriage, nor be there for you as you go through the process, the plain fact is that you can assemble your team from scratch. More about that later as we discuss building a winning team.

As you grow inside your shell and come out of it fortified, your newfound courage and authenticity will attract into your life supportive people who will make you feel invincible. Join a group of like-minded individuals, reach out to organizations and online communities of your peers.

And never underestimate the power of a competent therapist to support you as you contemplate whether to stay or go. Get yourself strong and healthy—whether you stay or exit. With the right support team in place, you will be able to successfully make—and carry out—your decision to leave or to stay.

Reflections
Do you feel supported by
the people in your life?

Whom can you trust and count on as you
decide the fate of your marriage?
Are they aware of your marital problems? If so,
how have they reacted?
If they are not supportive,
where else can you turn?
Investigate your options.
Make a list of viable support systems.
Reach out to one of them daily.

No Place to Go

This is a biggie. You can't get out of a miserable place if you have no other place to go. That's how I felt. My family lived thousands of miles away and I had no place to stay if I left my husband. I concealed my situation from my parents because I didn't want them to worry. After all, they could do nothing to help. And friends aren't always willing to open the doors to their homes to a runaway friend.

Unlike the lucky ones who can find a safe haven with loving relatives, I kept my woes to myself until I became strong enough to say it was over. I also realized that, if I didn't want to, I didn't have to go anywhere—that my home was supposed to be my haven.

If you have no friends or family you can stay with while you weather the storm, start investigating your housing options. Having such options will give you a sense of security and empowerment. Meanwhile, use the techniques offered in this book to strengthen yourself while you devise a viable exit strategy.

If you are in an abusive relationship, seek help from the police and get a protection order. No one should stay in an unsafe situation for lack of a place to go. Reach out to your local domestic violence organizations and find out if there are shelters in your area where you can stay until you can put together a safe escape plan.

Shame

Shame is the lowest and most destructive of all emotions. It is paralyzing. We all fear being judged. You may agonize about what people will think of you. Picking the wrong spouse is painful, but it's not the end of the world. If your social group has negative attitudes towards divorce, look for other individuals who have successfully freed themselves from similar situations for support.

If you torment yourself with thoughts of something you did in the past, this is the time to release it. We all do the best we can. If you made mistakes, own them, correct them, learn from them, and know that you can choose again. Let go of your feelings of shame and replace them with faith and the optimism that you have what it takes to turn things around.

Seek help from a trusted therapist and work through these issues if they are too painful or difficult to handle on your own.

Financial Dependence

Many people stay in unhappy marriages because they depend financially on their partners. They fear that they cannot earn enough money on their own or that they need two incomes to make ends meet. Perhaps they are afraid they can't survive if they have to split with their exes their pensions or other retirement benefits. Or they may have become used to an affluent marital lifestyle and would hate to give it up in a divorce.

I admit these are powerful considerations, but this is limited thinking. It's like staying in the job from hell for the health benefits, even though the job is making you sick.

Inevitably, a divorce will lead to supporting two households with the same money that supported just one. There will be two houses. The economies of scale will be lost, and there will be less money to go around. But that is only temporary. Your situation *will* change for the better if you put your mind and heart to it.

You must be thinking, "That's impossible. Absolutely pie in the sky." If you are, you must not know the story of motivational speaker and spiritual prosperity teacher Edwene Gaines. Edwene Gaines was a divorced, single mother—so strapped for cash that she used to dig in the sofa for pennies to give to her daughter to buy lunch. Many days they had no food in the house.

Yet, she intended to turn things around and, not only became a wealthy woman, but a prosperity teacher whose mission is to empower others and transform the abundance consciousness of Planet Earth. Edwene Gaines is in her seventies now, and still travels extensively, proclaiming the good news of prosperity for all—with tremendous zest and hot curlers in tow, to boot!

Her book, *The Four Spiritual Laws of Prosperity: A Simple Guide to Unlimited Abundance*, sold like hotcakes after she was mentioned in an article about Brazilian healer John of God that appeared in "O, The Oprah Magazine."

Edwene Gaines is a living testament that you can conquer your financial troubles with right thinking and right action. You can make it happen, too!

You may be deceived by appearances, but your spouse is not the source of your supply. You existed before you met. You inhabit a world of infinite possibilities, and you are a being of infinite potentiality. You have the power to increase your earning capacity and pursue the lifestyle of your dreams—if you're determined to change your circumstances.

You have the power to write your own ticket to joy, freedom and success! Once you have removed yourself from the circumstances that hold you back, you can harness your strength to create a brand-new future.

For an infusion of magical possibility and motivation, check out *The Success Principles: How to Get from Where You Are to Where You Want to Be* by Jack Canfield. This book has transformed my life! It offers 67 proven principles used by successful people that will help you achieve what you want—including financial freedom—no matter where you are in life in this moment.

Take a baby step today and start educating yourself about money matters. The Women's Institute for Financial Education (WIFE) offers fantastic financial literacy information about budgeting, investing and retirement to women in all stages of life—including divorce. Or book an appointment with a life or financial coach to help you dispel limiting beliefs and implement an abundance strategy.

Consider starting a business from your home for extra cash or a possible career change. You have so many options available to you! Begin researching them without delay!

Finally, keep in mind that your local divorce laws may favor you, and that you may receive financial support from your spouse while you get yourself back on your feet. Consult a legal services organization to better understand your rights and options.

Tap into every available source of information and inspiration and begin your journey of financial empowerment and liberation!

Reflections
Do you financially depend on your spouse?
Do you fear you can't support yourself?
Are you afraid that you won't have any money
left if you have to split your
assets with your spouse?

Are you unhappy enough that you are willing
to take the steps to provide
for yourself if you leave?
Is your current lifestyle sufficiently important
to you that you would be honestly happier
staying in an imperfect marriage?

Lack of Information

Some say ignorance is bliss, but it can also be a trap, especially for people locked in toxic relationships. Not knowing your rights and options will trick you into making life-altering decisions from a place of weakness. And oftentimes, our mates keep us blinded behind a veil of self-serving propaganda. It is not uncommon for people to stay in a prison of fear, under threats that their spouses will take the kids away, throw them out on the streets or get them deported.

Information is power. If your vision is clouded by pictures of doom painted by your spouse, get the correct information. The odds are he or she is bluffing to keep you under a spell. Seek counsel from a lawyer, a non-profit organization or other reputable sources. Research the questions that matter to you most. Armed with the proper information, you can examine your marriage and make the decision to leave or to stay from a position of wisdom.

Reflections
Is your spouse making threats
to scare you if you leave?
Are you certain they are true?
What if these threats are meritless,
with no basis in reality?
Would you stay with your partner knowing
these scare tactics are unfounded?

Lack of Education

In this day and age, you need skills to make a living. Perhaps you feel trapped because you lack the education and skills you believe are necessary to support yourself with dignity. That may be true—at this time. But you can enhance your employment skills.

You may not realize that you have other skills and personal qualities that make you a desirable employee. Having worked as a recruiter, I can honestly say that employers are willing to train people who are driven, hardworking and eager to learn and grow.

Research your dream job and find out what skills and training are necessary to perform its duties. Make friends with your local Unemployment or Department of Labor offices for help and career counseling. Get information about training programs designed to help people like yourself change careers and improve their skill sets.

Investigate classes offered at your local vocational schools and community colleges and look into adult education courses, grants and scholarships that may be available. Some organizations provide classes, such as English as a second language, for free. Stop by your library to find out more about the many options that could transform you into the confident employee any employer would be lucky to hire.

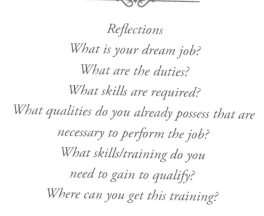

Reflections
What is your dream job?
What are the duties?
What skills are required?
What qualities do you already possess that are necessary to perform the job?
What skills/training do you need to gain to qualify?
Where can you get this training?

Religious Beliefs

Religion is a powerful force that often holds believers imprisoned in miserable marriages. Plenty of religious writings and dogma condemn divorce.

At the risk of sounding sexist, some religions mandate women to be submissive and subservient to men. As a result, these doctrines are inappropriately weaponized to keep women in abusive relationships or to make them tolerate despicable behaviors from their husbands. If your religion chastises or shuns women who divorce their husbands, you will be deterred from making a move necessary for your self-preservation.

But there's hope. Trust me. You see, I am a good Catholic-school girl, raised to get married and stay married. When I said, "I do," I vowed to stay with my husband for better or for worse. Yet I never expected "the worse" to mean accepting abusive behaviors. My common sense and self-respect told me I should not have to endure disrespect and abuse at the hands of my husband to be a decent person or a Catholic in good standing.

For many Catholics, both men or women, the stigma of divorce or the difficulties in obtaining an annulment deter unhappily married couples from seeking a divorce. I fully understand.

As a woman of faith, I made certain that I had honored my vows to the best of my ability, and leaving my husband was a decision I didn't make lightly. I was committed to fulfill my part of the bargain.

Nonetheless, my ex-husband used my faith as a license to engage in deplorable conduct and took every opportunity to rub in my face that I couldn't divorce because I was Catholic. He even had the audacity to offer to go along with an annulment if I admitted that I was crazy. Such coercive tactics are below the belt, and no one should be cornered to choose between dignity and freedom.

This happens to individuals of *all faiths*. Irrespective of your religion, you deserve to be happy and to be in a respectful relationship. Religious beliefs shouldn't be used as an excuse to mistreat you with impunity. If your faith is important to you, and you are not sure whether divorce is appropriate in your situation, seek guidance from a trusted member of your clergy. I was pleasantly surprised that the clergy I confided in supported my decision to leave. In fact, my parish priest told me emphatically and unequivocally to "*get out.*"

However, that isn't always the case, and we hear of clergy counseling people to remain in toxic relationships where they suffer physical and emotional harm. Talk to more than one person if you feel unsure, or if the person you first talked to didn't understand your situation, or if he or she seemed more concerned with dogma than with your safety and well-being.

The first time we went to a priest, my ex-husband lied to him convincingly and portrayed me as a crazy whore. I felt violated by my own religion when the priest disbelieved me and took sides with my then-husband. And this happens to many people, especially in conservative religious groups. However, this is a matter of utmost importance in your future and your spirituality, so do not give up on yourself. Get a second (or third) opinion from another member of the clergy.

If you don't feel supported by your community of faith, do not be afraid to seek counseling from a neutral therapist or local social services agency. The key is to get help to save *yourself and your faith* whether or not your marriage is viable.

Once you feel satisfied that you have done your part and that divorce is inevitable, religion should not be a barrier to ending an unhappy marriage and rebuilding both of your lives. Neither should divorce get in the way between you and your God. Do not give up on your faith because your decision to divorce is incompatible with dogma. Seek stillness, go within and tap into your inner guidance.

If you belong to a strict religion, in which leaving your spouse would put your life in danger or would entail renouncing your family and community ties, all the more reason to get help. Countless people have ended toxic marriages against unspeakable odds. Their examples can inspire you and infuse you with the courage you need to end the relationship that is ruining your life. If you are trying to flee from an arranged or forced marriage, Unchained at Last can help you escape and rebuild your life, even if your family has shunned you or forced you into hiding.

Reflections
What does your religion say about divorce?
Do these statements ring true?
What are your personal beliefs?
Do you believe God will punish you for leaving your spouse?
What fears, if any, come to your head when you consider divorce?
Condemnation? Or acceptance?

Guilt

The thought of leaving your spouse makes you feel badly. Do you feel guilty about something you did that you need to punish yourself for—by staying together? Do you feel like you deceived him or her in any way? Guilt is a very destructive emotion. Unprocessed feelings of guilt are incompatible with freedom and fulfillment.

Do your best to repair any mistakes of the past, but do not condemn yourself to eternal misery. Seek professional help, individually or as a couple.

And remember that your spouse doesn't have to be a terrible person for you to leave. You may simply be incompatible, and your life together feels dull and unsatisfying. If, after reasonable efforts, you and your partner can't turn things around, it is time to cut your losses, so that both of you can have a shot at being happy—albeit separately.

Reflections
Does the thought of leaving your spouse trigger feelings of guilt?
What do you feel guilty about?
Can you seek forgiveness?
If withheld, could you forgive yourself?
What actions can you take to repair the harm you've caused?

The Well-being of the Kids

You are afraid that divorce will ruin your children's lives. Worse—you fear that they will hate you for it, too. And you're willing to suffer quietly to avoid that catastrophe. Maybe your spouse is an excellent parent and provider. Or perhaps you come from a broken home and want your children to have what you wished for growing up.

You may not feel confident that you can raise the children on your own. Or you believe that a divorce, with its possible changes in homes and schools, will destroy their stability. You're a fine parent and don't want to deprive your children of those things you consider key to their well-being.

This is no slight matter, and it needs to be examined carefully and with an open mind. While, in an ideal world, happy parents raise happy children, psychologists say that staying together in a miserable marriage for the sake of the children doesn't do them any good.

Fighting and other behaviors that signal marital unrest will impress upon the children and will influence their choice of partners and affect their romantic relationships as they grow up. Even if you don't think the kids notice, or you don't fight in front of them, children are sensitive and can pick up on your cues, subtle as they may be.

A respectful divorce where the parents put their children's best interests above their differences might be a better option for all involved. Many couples become excellent co-parents. Maybe you and your spouse can make it happen. It is healthier for the kids to live with divorced parents who get along than with parents who stay together in a living hell for their "benefit."

A qualified therapist can assist you in making that hard decision based on the individual circumstances of your marriage and your children.

Educate yourself with the wisdom of these excellent books: *The Truth About Children and Divorce,* by Robert Emery and *For Better or For Worse: Divorce Reconsidered,* by E. Mavis Hetherington and John Kelly.

Reflections
Do you know how your children feel about
your relationship with your spouse?
Are you afraid they will take sides?
Underneath it all, is it about
you or about them?
How do you think your children
will react to a divorce?
Do they have special needs that will make a
divorce more difficult for them?
Do you and your spouse have the potential to
co-parent successfully?

Fear

There's no beating around the bush. Divorce is a scary business. It is full of uncertainty. You are probably plagued with a lot of fears.

Pondering the prospect of leaving your life partner is like opening a can of fear worms. Fear of the unknown. Fear of being alone. You may wonder, "What will my family say? What's going to happen? How will I survive a divorce? Is my soon-to-be-ex going to take me to the cleaners? Am I going to end up homeless? Will he or she take the kids away? Will I ever be loved again?"

The list of fears can be endless. Feeling such fears is natural. Some fears are totally irrational but not less powerful or paralyzing. However, you should not allow fear to hold you back from getting out of a situation that is already bad. You are unhappily married, remember?

The world opens up to magical possibilities when you're free from the misery of a destructive relationship. I am not suggesting that you recklessly leap into the unknown, but fear should not be the single factor keeping you trapped in what, after careful consideration, is an unsalvageable marriage.

Let me make this clear: under no circumstances should you stay in your marriage solely out of fear. It is a wondrous world out there—ready for you to discover.

Fear has been defined as False Evidence Appearing Real. Chances are many of your fears are unfounded and you need to tackle them head-on. Your life depends on it—literally.

In a later chapter, we will discuss fear in more detail, and we will do some exercises together to help you face *and* deface the fears that are holding you back from reconstructing your life—with or without a partner.

Reflections
What fears keep you in your relationship?
Are they real?
Do you have evidence that they are real?
Or are they're bluff designed
to keep you trapped?

I'm Too Old

This is a biggie. Totally laced with fear... many of them founded. Quite often old shoes stay in pairs because divorce during the mature years seems even more daunting than at a younger age.

There will be less money coming in if the parties are retired. Couples are living on fixed incomes and, dividing up the assets—pensions, 401(k)s and social security benefits— becomes more complex. No matter who pays the alimony—or who collects it—there will be less money to go around. The financial effects can be devastating.

And then there are the health issues. Older bodies tend to malfunction and require more medical care. Plus, for some, physical activity and leisure could be in decline.

It gets worse... what about recoupling? Can you fathom dating again and remarrying at "this age"? Will you be destined to live alone, with no one to rub on the Bengay?

Yet, surprisingly, "gray divorces" are on the rise. A 2017 report by the Pew Research Center revealed that the divorce rate for people over 50 doubled since the 1990s, while it tripled for people 65 and older between 1990 and 2015.

The good news is that, since people are living longer lives, a gray divorce comes with the opportunity to start anew at an age when they are more interested in enjoying themselves for the rest of their lives.

In fact, a survey conducted by the AARP showed that 76% of respondents who divorced later in life felt they made the right decision to end their marriages. Even more encouraging, respondents in their sixties and seventies reported appreciating their post-divorce lives the most!

The bottom line is that, not only do you deserve to be happy, but *you can be happy at any age!* With or without a partner. I have older friends who divorced or were widowed in their mature years, lead very active lives and are having a lot more fun than I am. Some are dating, some are unattached, but they're all living the dream.

Today is the first day of the rest of your life—staying married or getting divorced is a choice. You always have a choice. Don't let age be a barrier to making the choice that's right for you.

In Conclusion

Every one of the above reasons can keep you in a marriage in which you are not happy. They can cloud your judgment and trick you into sticking it out, even when your gut is telling you to leave. Remember that lots of people have left terrible marriages, even worse than yours. Some have overcome impossible odds. So can you.

In the chapters that follow, we will look at ways to make you stronger and more confident, so you, too, can beat the odds and create a fulfilling life—with or without a partner.

Is It Worth the Fight?

In deciding whether to stay, to keep trying or to run for the door, keep in mind the following considerations that can make or break your relationship.

Is Your Partner Clueless or Evil?

When we do things that hurt or annoy others, we usually do it out of ignorance, not with malice. The same may be true of your spouse. Have you considered whether your partner is aware of how this conduct hurts you?

Or are those actions so offensive that no reasonable, healthy person would inflict them on others? It is one thing to be mindless and inconsiderate and another to be mean and abusive. There is a huge difference between forgetting to flush the toilet and humiliating you.

Reflections
Make a list of your partner's annoying
behaviors and ponder if they would be
offensive to a reasonable person.
Are they mindless, reckless,
or do they seem intentional?
Have you discussed how those
behaviors affect you?
Is your partner open to
taking corrective action?

Is Your Spouse Up to the Challenge of Working Things Out?

After careful reflection, you will spot those thorny issues that put your marriage in danger. The next question is—is your spouse willing *and* able to work through these issues? Is he or she receptive to couples counseling?

As the saying goes, it takes two to tango. You cannot do your partner's emotional work any more than his or her workouts. So, if your other half has neither the desire nor the ability to team up with you to restore your relationship, you will end up feeling frustrated and alienated.

Remember, the fight to keep an unworkable marriage going is exhausting. It's a journey that you must take together, jumping over hurdles and picking yourselves up when you stumble and fall. No matter how genuine your intention to work things out, your marriage is not going to survive if your partner is not ready to go the extra mile with you.

Come to the Realization that Your Spouse May Never Get It

I hate to tell you, but this is a very distinct possibility. Your spouse may be convinced that he or she is in the right. That it's entirely *your* fault. If that's the case, there is nothing you can do to fix the mess.

Your partner grew up with as many incorrect beliefs and societal views as you. They could be so ingrained that he or she may be oblivious to odious conduct. So don't expect him or her to change.

These incompatibilities may be insurmountable, especially if you grew up in different environments, whether ethnic or socioeconomic. Be mindful that your spouse's views on men-women relationships and power dynamics may be at odds with yours.

Pay attention to his or her words. You may have taken them as idle chat or said in jest, but they reveal your spouse's innermost thoughts and beliefs. Some sexist comments that you find unacceptable or offensive may provide clues that your partner's mindset is fixed on an alternate reality that is never going to match yours.

In my ex-husband's culture, berating and controlling women was par for the course. His behaviors were inappropriate in our American society. To him, there was nothing wrong with telling me I was worth less than the dirt under his fingernail or with trying to make me feel low and undeserving.

As I walked out the door for the last time, his parting words were: "Maybe someday you will tell me the *real reasons* why you're leaving."

I rest my case.

Should You Stay Married or Should You Hit the Road?

Making the Decision from a Centered Place

Now that you've examined your relationship from every angle, it is time to do the math and make the hard decision to leave or to stay.

Deciding whether to leave an unsatisfying marriage or sticking it out is no small task. It's a major decision, as big as getting married, if not more. Therefore, never make it in haste or in the heat of an argument. Besides taking the time to do your exercises, you need a peaceful mind, so that your inner wisdom can bubble up and guide you into taking the right course.

Unfortunately, we are often consumed by obsessive thinking. The truth is that solutions cannot come into a mind cluttered with thought patterns of fear, anger, victimhood, revenge or any negative emotion. So, *please* review your journal entries and go over your answers to the reflections and exercises for insights. And, just as important, go back to the earlier sections in this book discussing intuition and meditation, to support you in making your decision from a position of strength, clarity and inner peace.

Congratulations!
You Got a Keeper

After all the soul searching and hard work, you may conclude that your spouse is a keeper. Congratulations. Sometimes what at first glance seems like an unhappy marriage can morph into a joyful relationship through the power of active awareness and right action.

I am happy to have shared with you this part of your personal journey and wish you the best in your relationship and blissful life ahead.

Keep this book handy for future reference and review the exercises in it from time to time, to keep you alert and on your toes. If you found it helpful, please share it with a friend who might enjoy it.

Continue to read on and indulge in the empowering practices ahead, which will enrich your life and make it more fulfilling with your spouse. The results will surprise you, as your life becomes more satisfying, and as you become a happier person and a more loving partner, parent, child and friend.

I wrote these empowering messages intending to help you discover your potential for happiness and well-being—in or out of your marriage.

Keep the momentum going and leave a review with your favorite online retailer, so that other unhappily married people can discover their inner power, get off the fence, and live fuller lives—with or without their mates.

Dropping the "D Bomb"

Announce Your Departure with Grace

You have done your homework. After much reflection you realize, not only how you got in, but that the only way is *out*. Your marriage is at a dead end, and you need to make it known.

Finally. The dreadful moment you have been preparing for has arrived. This is the time to have "the talk" and say it's over. It will be awkward, unpleasant, but it must be done. There is no way around it. You must feel confident that you're ready and able to handle this conversation. This isn't the time to botch it. So take time to center yourself and muster the serenity and strength you will need.

This was the hardest thing for me. I was terrified to tell my ex-husband I was done and dreaded the night of tears and loneliness that would follow the conversation. Having no place to go and no one to be with, I avoided it altogether.

Then, one night he went through my car and found the divorce complaint I had hidden under the driver's seat. I couldn't avoid it anymore. There were tears, there was a lump in my throat, but I transcended it and spoke my truth. Just like that. And I slept through the night. I overcame the dreaded feelings of loneliness. And I didn't die. I actually felt relieved.

You can't choreograph, stage or rehearse your exit speech. You can't time it with the precision of a Swiss watch. But you must prepare for this moment and, unless you have pre-selected the conditions, you must be ready to seize the opportunity when it arises.

If you're lucky, your spouse will give you an opening— engage in that unacceptable behavior you can't stand, or drop the last straw, so to speak. If you'd rather have control over the situation, you can pick a time and place that are more comfortable for you.

This conversation is of utmost importance. It is your chance to, at long last, say your piece. It is the first outward step towards your liberation and sets the tone for your divorce.

Below are some guidelines to help you get ready to exit with dignity and poise.

Be Prepared

I can't overemphasize how important it is to be mentally prepared for this life-altering step. Even though there's no script for this tough conversation, you still need to think it through ahead of time. Unless you're thrown into this situation at an inopportune moment, it pays off to take the time and effort to do your inner work, explore your options, and feel empowered to make this move correctly before you embark on the divorce journey.

- Be centered and serene.
- Spend some time quieting the mind and visualize yourself speaking confidently and without hesitation.
- Know what you want to say.
- Decide in advance what you want to achieve from the conversation. (Do you want to move out? Have you found a place to stay? Do you have a lawyer?)
- You don't know how your spouse will react, so expect the unexpected.

Be Sensitive

This is tough stuff. You will be telling the love of your life that you don't want to be with him or her anymore. This hurts you, I know, and it will hurt your spouse, too. That's why, in the name of the love you once had for each other, it is critical to be sensitive despite the emotional baggage accumulated during your relationship.

Ending your marriage will require the delicate balance of honoring yourself and being kind. As in every area of your life, practicing the golden rule will set the tone for your separation or, at the very least, create some good karma.

Ask yourself how you would like to be treated if the roles were reversed. Besides the inevitable feelings of rejection, would you like to be inflicted with humiliation and blame?

No matter how tempting—or how true—this is not the time to tell your wife that you hate her guts, to tell your husband you're repulsed by his beer belly or to declare that your mother-in-law is the greatest witch on the planet. Although this may be the culmination of years of misery, and the confession may appear cathartic, letting it all out unfiltered may backfire, and right off the bat create a revenge-thirsty adversary determined to make your divorce hell. This is setting yourself up for failure and will set you back from your ultimate goals: freedom and fulfillment.

In the spirit of a peaceful resolution, break the news in a productive way. This is not something you do on a post-it note, in front of friends or family (especially the children) or during a heated argument.

Select a quiet, safe location where you can speak privately and without interruptions. Avoid the possibility of a public scene that would cause embarrassment or could escalate.

Be direct and sincere but not ambivalent. Your partner needs to understand you have carefully considered leaving, and that this is not something you're doing on a whim.

Make your speech short, sweet and to the point. Stick to the facts and avoid editorializing, as tempting as this may be.

Allow Time to Digest the News

Let's face it. All of us can be clueless. No matter how odious the behaviors, your spouse may not have seen this coming. Isn't that one of the reasons why you're leaving?

A man I know told my current husband that, after five kids and 25 years of marriage, his wife "woke up one day and decided she didn't want to be married anymore." And he believed it! And my husband believed it, too! I bet you dollars to donuts that the signs were there and that the wife told this fool he was being a jerk—for the previous 25 years!

Likewise, your spouse may not expect or may not understand your burning desire to jump ship. You may have caught him or her off guard and may fire back with excuses or blame.

Now is not the time to do the tit-for-tat. Listen attentively but make it clear that you've made up your mind and give your partner a chance to process the news. Once you announce your decision, you can resume the conversation when you are both calm and ready to begin sorting out the next steps.

Be Patient with Yourself

You need to be kind to yourself, too, and be open to the possibility that you will experience grief. Allow yourself to be surprised by your feelings. You may feel sadness or intense relief. Stay with your feelings and let them be there without judgment. Do not run away from your feelings and avoid the temptation to cover them up with distractions. You need to process them, too. You will have time to take action afterwards.

Are You Open to Reconciliation?

Give your spouse a chance to speak, yet firmly express that you have made up your mind. Do not give him or her hope if there are no prospects for reconciliation.

If you're open to reconciliation, pause and wait for a response. If asked for another chance, have a mental list of your demands, and make it understood that you won't settle for less.

Again, you must determine what you need to be happy in the marriage before you begin this conversation. What changes would persuade you to stay married? Couples counseling? More help around the house? More support? End of inconsiderate, hurtful behaviors? More space? Go back to your journal and review your list of relationship must-haves.

Give your spouse a reasonable deadline to correct the problem areas to avoid wasting your life in a hopeless relationship. Let your spouse know you're willing to try again—*if* he or she steps up to the plate.

Keep Your Eyes on the Prize: Freedom

Your spouse may have tormented you for years, but this is not the time for thoughtful reciprocity. This conversation will set in motion the divorce process. Keep your eyes on the prize and remember at all times that you want to start your life from scratch. And to accomplish that, it is in your best interest to get the deed done as efficiently as possible. You want to set the stage for what you hope will be a cordial, respectful process.

Remember–Your Spouse Will Get Over It

This is hard, I know, and you may even experience pity. But the bottom line is that your spouse will eventually get over it. Sooner or later. Do not beat yourself up or stay in the trap of the unhappy marriage because your partner starts acting pathetic. Time heals all wounds.

Above All: Be Safe

Staying safe in a volatile situation is your number one concern. Use sound judgment. If your partner has mental health problems, is aggressive or if you're afraid the situation will turn violent, take precautions.

Have this conversation in a secure location—never in the car or in a solitary place. Avoid areas where your spouse will have access to weapons, such as knives, tools or firearms. Stay away from the top of the stairs and rooms without access to an outside exit, in case you need to flee.

And do not be afraid to call for help if you believe you are in danger. Keep your cell phone and the phone number of the police department handy.

Breaking up is the most dangerous stage in an abusive relationship. Plan a safe escape in advance and make

PART III

KEEPING THINGS AMICABLE

A Little Kindness
Goes a Long Way

"Be kind whenever possible. It is always possible." The Dalai Lama

I know what you're thinking... How can I ask you to be kind when your spouse is being a jerk? You don't feel like being kind to someone who makes your life hell.

As ironic as this may seem, the more of a jerk your partner is, the greater the reason to be kind. In the heat of the moment, it may feel cathartic to let it all out. But losing your cool will make a situation worse. Here is where kindness comes in.

Kindness is the art of responding from your highest self. Having dominion over your emotions and responses. Kindness makes *you* the boss. *You* put the ego in check and out of the driver's seat, while your highest self becomes the master of the situation.

Kindness is resisting the temptation to fire back and instead stepping back. It's ending the argument before it begins.

When your partner is trying to provoke a fight, or does something that pushes your buttons, step back and let your inner sage handle the situation. I'm not suggesting that you be a doormat but to be in control—*you* choose how you will respond to the unpleasant stimulus.

Kindness is awareness in action. Develop the wisdom to get out of a nasty situation unscathed, and—even better—to stay away altogether from situations likely to go bad. It can be as simple as saying a *sincere* and even-tempered, "I'm sorry. I didn't realize that… How can I fix it? Thanks for bringing it up. I will keep that in mind."

A simple way to practice kindness is to do something thoughtful without being asked, like picking up at the supermarket one of your husband's favorite treats or buying your wife flowers "for no reason."

Kindness is disarming. Have you ever been enraged over a situation, only to have the other person—manager, employee—smile and offer to fix it? What did that do to you? I bet it knocked you off your horse and made you put down your sword.

Similarly, acting kindly towards your spouse will probably take him or her by surprise. He or she will not see it coming and may be taken aback. The shock will give him or her, too, the opportunity to step back, instead of firing back. After all, you seek resolution and improved communication, particularly in high conflict situations.

Whether you stay together or divorce, kindness will help you stay sane and serene, so your actions align with what's best for all.

Kindness keeps you centered and calm. You will feel better. You retain your power when you don't allow yourself to get dragged into reactivity, escalating a situation and saying things you will regret. Kindness stops you from continuing the argument in your head for hours—stewing over the things said and playing over and over the things you would have liked to say.

If your partner doesn't respond to kindness, you have your answer. You probably are in a no-win situation. Not responding to kindness with kindness signals that your partner is incapable or unwilling to look at things differently and bring about positive changes. Your partner has some healing to do, but you can't force him or her to enlightenment.

Peter, my current husband, exemplified the practice of kindness when we first got together, and I was instantly smitten by his kind heart. During our first years together, we rarely fought, and most disagreements ended with, "How can we fix this?"

I admit that, over the years, we have both fallen off the kindness wagon, and we need to jump back on. But we have agreed to discuss issues calmly before they turn into fights, and we share the commitment to becoming more patient with each other.

You can continue to choose again and again until you develop the habit of responding to every situation with kindness. It is a skill worth perfecting.

If you don't believe me, start practicing with other people. Then you can try it with your spouse. Living in a constant state of kindness is not easy and takes practice and patience.

We are conditioned to instinctively fight back, compliments of our reptilian brain and our social conditioning.

Congratulate yourself on every victory and catch yourself when you slip up. Look back and investigate why you fell off the wagon and keep track of the situations that trigger unkindness reactivity.

Reflections
What events, situations and emotions
cause you to go on reactivity mode?
Use your journal as your biographer and look for patterns that
reveal what you need to work on.
How do you feel when you choose to act from kindness?
Do you have feelings of resistance to being kind to your spouse?
Do something nice for your spouse today—for no reason.

Forgiveness:
The Portal to the Future

"There is no future without forgiveness." Desmond Tutu

Whether you are exploring the viability of your marriage or on the path to divorce, forgiveness is the foundation of your personal liberation. Over the course of your marriage, you and your partner must have said and done things that were hurtful and toxic. Perhaps you resent your spouse for leaving your marriage if you wished to stay together. Hanging on to these hurts will perpetuate their destructive effect unless—and until—you release them.

Hanging on to past hurts is like strapping an anchor to your neck and dragging it wherever you go. Unforgiveness will bring you down and prevent you from rising to your highest potential. It will deprive you of the peace that you need to create a joyful life. You won't be able to start over with a clean slate if you're still obsessed with the wrongs of the past.

When you forgive, you release yourself from the bondage of blame and resentment and break free from the spell past hurts have placed on you.

Forgiveness is freedom from judgment, ill feelings, and being "right" at the expense of being happy. Sometimes we adopt a posture of righteous indignation because we mistakenly believe that not forgiving the other person makes him or her the bad guy, while making us the victim, the nice guy. We feel morally superior.

Being unforgiving doesn't make you good and the other person bad. It makes *you* unhappy! The other person goes on with his or her life untouched by your anger and hatred.

Remember: you deserve to be happy. So tap into the power of forgiveness to set yourself free. You need to forgive your spouse for every wrong—real or perceived. Yes—every single one of them. You need to forgive yourself for all the things you regret associated with your marriage and in every area of your life.

You need to forgive every person who, in your opinion, contributed to the breakdown of your marriage. That includes friends, relatives, in-laws, even "the other" man or woman.

This is hard stuff, I know, and don't get mad at me for saying so. But as hard as this may be, it is essential to *your happiness*. Release the charge. Stop thinking about it, or at least think about it with neutral feelings.

We are often unwilling to forgive because we assume that forgiving turns us into doormats. That forgiving is condoning offensive behaviors. That, by forgiving, we are making them acceptable. We are enabling the perpetrator. We are inviting more of the same.

But that isn't true. Forgiving is not about condoning offensive behaviors. Some behaviors, abusive ones in particular, are wrong and unacceptable and you should never tolerate them.

Those behaviors may give you powerful reasons to end your marriage. But they do not justify ending your peace and depriving yourself of the happiness that is your birthright. Forgiveness opens the door to a life of freedom and possibility. Forgiveness makes room in your heart to allow love to flow in.

Maybe you're not comfortable forgiving because you fear it makes you seem weak. To the contrary, forgiving is empowering, because it dissolves the grip past hurts have over you. It allows you to face your vulnerabilities and gives you the opportunity to heal and dissolve them.

You see, when you hang on to past hurts and resentments, you are giving your power away to the other person. Holding on to resentment poisons *you*. It keeps you bound to the person you badly want out of your life.

Every time you think about the hurtful event, you are allowing it to continue hurting you over and over again—even after the conduct has stopped. Some people hang on to hurts that happened long ago, by people who may no longer be alive. Who do you think is hurt by the unforgiveness? Not the dead guy, for sure!

You are not alone. We have all been hurt, often by people we love. By people we thought loved us. And we have to process feelings of betrayal as well.

Perhaps you have endured vicious behaviors that were uncalled for. You think you have been inflicted the unforgivable. I understand.

I am not trying to minimize your pain. But open your mind to the possibility that other people have endured horrifying experiences, even worse than yours, and have found it in their hearts to forgive. Through forgiveness, these people have achieved freedom, and they inspire us to invite the power of forgiveness to heal our deepest wounds.

Louise Hay was sexually abused as a child. Yet, she turned her painful experiences into an occasion to heal herself and to help others heal through a lifetime of inspiring works. Likewise, Immaculee Ilibagiza, in her book *Left to Tell: Discovering God in the Midst of the Rwandan Holocaust*, shares her stirring story on achieving freedom through forgiveness, after her family members were murdered by friends and neighbors during the genocide in Rwanda in the 1990s. Their examples underscore how forgiveness can serve *you*.

Forgiveness doesn't stop with your spouse. Also, forgive yourself. The past is over and done. You cannot change it, but you can choose again. Learn your lessons and become a better person from it.

Consider incorporating a forgiveness practice into your life. It will support you as you examine your relationship, decide whether to leave or to stay and as you try to pick up the pieces and rebuild your life when your marriage ends. Forgiveness is the cornerstone of your future—with or without your spouse. It will pay dividends in every area of your life and will enable you to enjoy healthier relationships and a serene existence.

If you're not sure how to do it, there is plenty of help available. The subject is so vast and complex that you could fill an entire library with books about forgiveness. There are lots of amazing teachers, all of them courageously sharing their personal stories and unique forgiveness techniques. Find one that resonates with you. Or feel free to create techniques of your own if you can't find one that is right for you.

My favorite book on the subject is *Forgiveness: 21 Days to Forgive Everyone for Everything* by Iyanla Vanzant. This fabulous little book comes with a built-in 21-day workbook and includes a CD with guided meditation exercises for every day of your forgiveness journey. By day 14, I felt considerably lighter and more peaceful.

I have also found inspiration in Louise Hay's book *You Can Heal Your Life*, and Colin Tipping's *Radical Forgiveness: Making Room for the Miracle*. You can even join forgiveness support groups at a local church or online.

The key is to allow the power of forgiveness to release you from the wounds of the past and pave the way for a brighter future.

If You're Not Ready to Forgive Yet

Maybe your spouse or others have engaged in damaging behaviors that you need to process. Perhaps your emotions are still raw, and you are not yet ready to forgive. Be kind to yourself and honor your feelings.

Forgiveness requires you to be ready and receptive. You may wish to wait until the heat is off, the dust settles, and you are out of the emotional danger zone. That is perfectly okay.

Take baby steps down the road to forgiveness. Louise Hay taught that you could start by being *willing* to forgive. Take the first step now and rejoice in a life in which your spouse's misdeeds are not even worthy of a passing thought.

Now you're ready to begin anew. Rebuild your life on a clean slate with the power of forgiveness.

Forgiveness Exercise

Here's a technique I used effectively to process the nasty behaviors my ex-husband inflicted on me. List everything you can remember that your spouse did to you that still hurts or stings. Keep writing until you can't think of anything else to add to the list. Then write a letter to your spouse letting him or her know how each of those actions made you feel. Tell him or her you are not condoning those behaviors but that you choose to release the pain, because you deserve to be happy, and you want to set yourself free.

After you finish writing the letter, burn it. Drink a glass of water and engage in physical activity to clear the energy out of your body. Go for a brisk walk, hit the gym or sing an uplifting song at the top of your lungs. Just do whatever makes you feel empowered and free.

If this exercise is too painful, stay away from the most hurtful experiences and begin with less hurtful ones. You can repeat this exercise as many times as needed until you process all your hurts.

Or begin by forgiving other people whose behaviors have hurt you in the past until you fortify your forgiveness muscle and perfect your forgiveness practice.

Letting Go:
The Cornerstone of Healing

Whether you and your spouse stay together or go on your separate ways, you can't move forward in freedom unless you let go of those thoughts and expectations that keep you tangled to the past or to a future that will never materialize.

Accept your circumstances, learn your lessons and let go. Hanging on will bring you additional disappointment and will prevent you from beginning a fresh life.

Dr. Wayne Dyer said that, "When you change the way you look at things, the things you look at change." Looking at your marriage in a different light opens up a world of possibility.

Attachment to any thing, person or outcome brings suffering, because losing it, or just the fear of losing it, makes you unhappy.

The important lesson here is that you cannot rebuild your life until you come to terms with the situation you are currently in and let go of the attachments. Attachments to what happened, to what you think should have happened, to what never happened. Attachments to the person you used to love, or who you hoped he or she would become.

Resisting "what is" is the root of suffering. Simply stated, you can't grab new blessings if your hands are hanging on to baggage. As long as you hold on to the disappointments, mistakes and hurts of the past, you won't be able to accept a future of unlimited possibility.

Likewise, self-recrimination and regret won't change what happened in the past, so you also need to release them. Living trapped in a space of regret over the things you did, the things you didn't do, or the opportunities missed won't bring you peace nor fix what went wrong in your relationship.

Make peace with your situation and release it.

Let Go of Dreams

You need to let go of the dreams and hopes you created around your relationship and, instead, open the door to new opportunities that can come into your life only if you are emotionally free.

It is a tough thing to do; I know. For me, it was hard to imagine an alternative life, and the fears of the unknown paralyzed me. I couldn't imagine dating other men or giving up on the future I had envisioned for myself. It is impossible to embrace a fresh life when you're hung up on what could have been or, more importantly, what you think "should have been."

But if I hadn't made the move, I might still be stuck in a bitter marriage, with all the lack and limitation that came with it. And because I was finally able to let go, I opened the way to an amazing life, with a recent husband and blessings I never imagined.

Reflections
What were your dearest dreams surrounding
your marriage?
Which of those dreams do
you still feel attached to?
Can you let them go?
What exciting dreams—
as a free agent—could replace them?

Let Go of Wrongs

Similarly, it is just as easy to hang on to the wrongs done and embellish them with thoughts of revenge. But what good is it? I know a woman who is still seething over her ex-husband's infidelities. And guess what? He has moved on. He has a new love in his life while she is alone with her anger. Wouldn't it be more productive to direct that energy towards creating a life of bliss for herself where her ex-husband is not even a thought?

When you fixate on what's wrong, you won't notice anything else around you, including what's good and worthy.

Reflections
Are there any past wrongs that keep you
entangled with your spouse?
Why do you hang on to them?
What juice are you getting from
hanging on to these wrongs?
Who would you be without them?

Let Go of the Past

Make no mistake—the past is over and done and cannot be changed. Dr. Wayne Dyer advised to let go of the notion that you can have a better past. How true. Take one last look at what happened, reflect on the lessons learned and don't look back. The future is ahead. Free your hands from baggage and make room for the blessings that await you.

Let Go of Your Mistakes

Perhaps, at some level, you feel guilt for some conduct you have engaged in that caused harm to your spouse or your relationship. We all make mistakes. Can you forgive yourself for your mistakes? Can you ask for forgiveness for those mistakes? Are you willing to make amends?

There is no benefit to living with regret and self-recrimination. Seek forgiveness, make amends where feasible and release the charge of past mistakes. Forgiving yourself and looking to the future with the resolve not to repeat these mistakes is the key out of your emotional prison cell.

Reflections
What mistakes have you committed in your
marriage that you regret deeply?
Can you fix them, forgive
yourself and let them go?

Let Go of Attachments

You are not served either by an attachment to an unlikely script in which you and your spouse live happily ever after. It feels comfortable and familiar to cling to a fantasy in which your spouse is the perfect partner, not the tormentor who makes your life miserable.

But, if you've done everything possible on your end, living that script would require your spouse to change. And you cannot change him or her. You can only change yourself.

Accepting the limitations of your partner and your relationship are essential to starting over. It is also essential to acknowledge and accept your own limitations that prevent you from living up to your partner's expectations, so you can live with authenticity.

Accepting and Blessing What Is

If, after careful reflection, you conclude that your marriage is not salvageable, you need to accept it and move on.

Life will not happen until you recognize that this relationship is not the path to the happiness you envisioned. To the happiness you deserve.

Once you come to terms with it, you can objectively view your marriage as a steppingstone that led you to where you are now. It is your springboard to the future, all the wiser for it, grateful for all its lessons and opportunities.

You attracted your spouse into your life for a reason. Reframe your situation and learn to see him or her as a teacher who taught you a lesson necessary for your personal evolution. Be grateful for the lessons and thank your partner in your mind. Then release your partner and your marriage and bless them both with love.

It is now time to heal. The best is yet to come.

Your Kids Deserve to Be Happy, Too

A Few Words for the Divorcing Parent

Divorce is difficult for you. But it is just as difficult for your children, if not more. They, too, are living with uncertainty and have fears of their own. They, too, are concerned about losing their parents and changing neighborhoods and going to schools where they have no friends. If they are very young, they may not understand what is happening or may be afraid that this debacle is their fault.

As you navigate the stormy waters of divorce, remember that their welfare comes first. Keep their well-being in mind as you make decisions that affect them. Listen to them and be supportive of their feelings. Reinforce that, even though you and your spouse do not get along and decided to separate, it is not their fault. Let them know, through your words *and* actions, that you love them very much.

Consider adding to your divorce team a mental health professional to help the children cope with the stresses of your separation. Before you do so, check the prospective therapist's credentials carefully. Talk to a collaborative lawyer or family court staff and make sure the therapist you select has extensive training and expertise in high conflict resolution. Or contact the Association of Family and Conciliation Courts (AFCC) for a referral.

At the risk of sounding like your mother, here is some advice that you may not think you need or that applies to you. But listen anyway.

No matter how tempting, do not use your children as pawns. We see this too often in divorce cases, and the children are the ones who get hurt.

Avoid disparaging your soon-to-be-ex. Your kids love both of their parents. Respect your children's feelings towards your spouse and do not sabotage their relationship. This will hurt your children and will ultimately hurt you, too, as your children grow up and realize that you manipulated them.

Avoid dramatic scenes in front of the kids. Do not fight in front of them. You are stressing them out. If your visitation exchanges are likely to get nasty, drop off or pick up the children at a neutral place. Or have a trusted relative be present, preferably someone who gets along with your spouse.

This is not the time to get into arguments. It will make the children dread spending time with the other parent, and it will make them unhappy. And, like you, they deserve to be happy.

Your lawyer or therapist can offer you suggestions that have worked well in other cases. The most important thing is to protect your children's safety and well-being.

Divorce Demystified

Legal proceedings are an inevitable part of the divorce journey. Perhaps the most distasteful, too.

Sadly, our understanding (or misunderstanding) of the divorce process comes from unreliable sources, like the movies and TV and the disasterpaloozas our parents, friends and relatives have endured.

Everybody seems to have a horror story to tell: "My lawyer screwed me." "My husband is a monster." "My wife took me to the cleaners."

But the bottom line is that the legal formalities are a mandatory rite of passage to freedom and that, ultimately, you will survive them. The better you understand the process, the easier you will navigate them and the higher your odds for a smooth sailing.

What I am offering you below is a simple overview of the legal process, so you can understand what's at stake and how you can prepare yourself to make informed decisions.

Please, be mindful that *every situation is unique* and that you will need *some* degree of legal guidance to protect your rights and your children's.

I'm not saying this to scare you or to peddle legal professionals like myself. I wish to protect you from cheating yourself of your best future and prevent you from making mistakes that will hurt you or your loved ones.

The section below does not constitute legal advice and is not intended to be a substitute for legal advice. Rather, it is meant to be an eye-opening exercise to help you understand what you're up against and why you need competent representation that is appropriate for your *individual* situation.

What's at Stake

Every decision you make in the divorce process affects the quality of your life, your spouse's and your children's now and in the future, so you need to consider them carefully. Consequently, preparedness is essential.

Again, to make wise decisions, you must understand what's at stake and what the process entails.

Divorce entails, not only the dissolution of your marriage, but other related matters, like:

- Property distribution – how your assets and debts will be split up between you and your spouse.

- Spousal support – whether one of the parties will need financial support, the appropriate amount and duration.
- Matters related to your children – establishing custody and parenting time for the school year, school breaks and holidays, as well as child support, which includes dividing expenses for health and education and others.

There are other details you may haven't considered, such as:

- Health insurance during and post-divorce.
- Division of retirement and public benefits, including social security, retirement accounts and pensions.
- Insurance policies to protect your property and to pay for obligations established in the divorce settlement agreement, in case the payor dies or becomes disabled.
- Estate planning – updating your wills and creating trusts.
- Bankruptcy.
- Personal injury awards.

How these issues play out is in turn affected by a series of factors, like the length of the marriage, the age and physical and emotional health of the parties, current economic circumstances, educational levels and earning abilities.

And then, some of those decisions that impact your everyday life can't wait until the divorce is over, including living arrangements, paying bills and day-to-day decisions affecting your children.

So, you and your spouse must make an agreement addressing the temporary workings of those key issues or have the court decide for you.

Where you live also plays a big role. The laws are different in every jurisdiction. Every country and states within a country can have different laws that affect every aspect of divorce. That's why you must be aware of how those laws will apply to your personal circumstances.

Uninformed decisions and poor planning can have an adverse effect on your tax liabilities, eligibility for public benefits and immigration status, among others.

And, under most circumstances, poor decisions regarding the division of property cannot be undone after the divorce is final.

As you can see, the issues can be many and complex. A couple with no children, no assets and no liabilities could quickly end things and go their separate ways.

But things are different for couples with children, lots of assets and special needs. The specifics of your case determine the issues that need resolution.

Your case may also require help from several professionals, like realtors, estate lawyers, insurance brokers, financial experts and mental health professionals, to educate you, guide your decisions and handle the details.

Obviously, the more things to fight about and the feistier the parties, the more complicated and prolonged the case will become. Some people can put their differences aside and reach a settlement that's in everyone's best interest. That's what every divorcing couple should strive for.

And then there's people who just want to fight. Your spouse may be one of them. Unfortunately, there's little you can do to change that. But here's a reminder: just as it takes two to tango, it takes two to fight.

Factor in the above considerations and choose the legal representative and model best suited to your situation.

Keeping Things Amicable: Selecting the Right Divorce Model

Keeping a divorce amicable is challenging, and there will be times when you'll wonder if it is possible or if it is worth it. There are no guarantees, but it is worth a try.

Even with the best of intentions, communications sometimes break down and spouses with unhealed issues may allow their anger and frustration to take over the divorce process. While complex situations present more issues to fight about, some people want to fight to cause pain, even where there is little at stake.

I hope that doesn't happen to you.

This section explains the various divorce models. Each of them offers the potential for parties to amicably end their marriage, so they can rebuild their lives with as little damage as possible.

Talk to your spouse early in the process to select the model most beneficial to you and your family.

Litigation

Most divorces go through litigation. In litigation, the parties go to court and ask a judge to decide their case. The parties present their requests and evidence and arguments supporting those requests. The judge then issues a ruling regarding the issues in dispute.

A litigated case is subject to a series of court rules and procedures the parties must follow and a timeline for each step in the process.

At the onset, the parties go through what is known as discovery, and are required to exchange information related to any issues they are asking the court to resolve.

Ideally, the parties can be cooperative and freely exchange such information.

Even better, the parties could cut to the chase and reach an agreement on those issues, instead of having a judge decide for them.

Unfortunately, negotiations often hit snags that need the court's intervention.

The result is that your divorce is now subject to court schedules and potential delays and, worse, a trial with a battle of experts that can extend your suffering and prevent you from moving on.

Anyone who's been through a toxic litigation is likely to have a horror story to share, with good reason. Litigation is painful and expensive.

But it doesn't have to be that way. Your attorneys can help you resolve your divorce and avoid a lengthy and acrimonious process.

Do not put your future and the well-being of your family in the hands of a stranger. Even the best judge doesn't know you or your family intimately and doesn't know what's best for you. Having a judge decide your case should be a last resort.

Collaborative Divorce

Collaborative divorce is a gentler legal model that focuses on cooperation and minimizes discord.

It gives the parties control over their divorce, incorporates emotional support to the couples and their families, and includes financial guidance to help them maximize their financial position to manage two separate households with the resources that used to support just one.

Collaborative divorce reduces the acrimony that characterizes litigation, giving couples a better chance to transition from the end of their marriage to a fresh life.

In collaborative divorce, the parties commit in advance to resolving their differences amicably and out of court. They also agree to freely exchange the information necessary to arrive at a fair settlement.

The collaborative process involves confidential meetings with a team of professionals trained to help the parties solve their issues in their best interests. The parties are represented at these meetings by their respective collaborative attorneys. They can also include neutral professionals who assist with the non-legal aspects of the divorce according to their needs.

For example, the divorce coach is a mental health professional who helps the spouses with the emotional aspects of the separation and in determining the best alternatives for the children.

The financial advisor helps the parties analyze their economic situation and offers solutions to make the most of their assets, divvy up liabilities and optimize their finances upon dissolution and beyond.

The collaborative model avoids long, costly and emotionally taxing legal battles and protects the children's welfare.

Once the parties reach an agreement, they sign the divorce papers, and their lawyers present them to the court so the divorce judgment can be issued.

Mediation

Mediation is a popular method to negotiate a divorce settlement out of court. In mediation, the parties meet with a neutral third party, called a mediator, to discuss and resolve the issues in the divorce. Their agreement is then formalized and incorporated into their divorce judgment.

Mediators are usually lawyers, retired judges or mental health professionals trained to assist divorcing couples in resolving their disputes. Their qualifications can vary widely, so choose with care.

The mediator doesn't represent the interests of either party or decide for them. Instead, he or she facilitates their settling the case without advocating for, or providing legal counsel to, either spouse.

Mediation is preferable to litigation. It is less costly and painful for the parties. It is an excellent model for couples with uncomplicated situations and a solution-oriented mindset.

However, if you're considering mediation, you must understand that the mediator is a neutral professional, not your lawyer nor an advocate charged with protecting your interests.

So, technically, a mediator may help you craft an agreement you are comfortable with but may not be an optimal outcome in your situation. If you have not received adequate counseling, you may agree to terms that are not good for you.

That's why, unless the issues are simple and few, the parties should consider bringing their respective attorneys to mediation to protect their interests and avoid accepting unfavorable terms.

Having attorneys present makes mediation more expensive, a factor you need to consider when selecting your divorce model.

For your protection, have an attorney review the agreement before signing it. You must make sure it is properly drafted and enforceable in court, in case your spouse does not comply with it after the divorce is completed.

Arbitration

Arbitration is another form of alternative dispute resolution.

Depending on your jurisdiction, the court may order your case to go to arbitration if previous negotiations have failed and you and your spouse can't come to an agreement. However, you may choose to go straight to arbitration.

In arbitration, the parties and their lawyers select an arbitrator who conducts a private trial out of court and issues a binding decision regarding the specific issues in dispute.

Arbitration has some advantages. It allows you to resolve your case more quickly, since you're not at the mercy of a backlogged court calendar.

It can also be less expensive, as you and your spouse don't have to pay your attorneys for time spent waiting in the courtroom for your case to be called. And, since you select the issues you want the arbitrator to decide, you can stipulate to the facts (meaning putting on the record the facts you agree on) and limit the issues before the arbitrator to those you could not resolve. In contrast, a court trial would require the attorneys to build a record and present evidence on all issues in the case, not just those in dispute, which adds to your aggravation and legal expenses.

Moreover, arbitration is a private proceeding, so your dirty laundry won't be aired in public, unlike a court trial.

Arbitration, however, comes with a disadvantage you must consider carefully when deciding how to go about your divorce. The arbitrator makes a binding decision, which means if you don't like it you will have to live with it. So the parties lose control over the decision and take the risk that the arbitrator, like a judge, may make decisions that are not optimal for them.

El Cheapo Divorce - At Your Own Peril

Not everybody has the money to pay for a divorce. For some couples, the cost of a standard divorce may exceed the value of their assets. So you may feel tempted to do it yourself.

Or you spot a billboard advertising the $350 divorce, and you become convinced that you should pay no more. Think again. And read the fine print. Common wisdom says you get what you pay for.

Be smart and ask what you get for your $350, including:

- What services does it cover?
- Who provides these services?
- What kind of counsel and support do you receive throughout the divorce process?

Typically, these cheap divorces include the preparation of divorce forms, so *you* can submit them to the court and serve them on your spouse. They are often drafted by paralegals, not attorneys. And, for that price, you are unlikely to receive a thorough review of your case and the legal counsel you need to understand your rights and make informed decisions.
Proceed with caution!

If money is a problem, seek help. There may be low-cost alternatives available to you. Contact your local courthouse for referrals to legal services organizations and legal clinics hosted by local law schools or charitable agencies. They may offer basic legal advice, explain your rights and/or help you represent yourself, if appropriate in your situation.

At the very least, consult an attorney to get an explanation of your rights and the divorce process in your jurisdiction.

You should also have a lawyer draft or review your divorce agreement to ensure it covers all bases and that it is enforceable. A poorly drafted homemade settlement could cost you dearly if you find out later—when you need it to work—that it is invalid.

You can always hire a lawyer to review your divorce settlement. In fact, mediators often work with lawyers to "sign off" on settlement agreements. But be clear: the services may be limited to ensuring the sufficiency of the document. In other words, the reviewing attorney verifies that the necessary clauses are contained in it and that the agreement is enforceable—not that it is the best deal for you.

Even a legally sufficient document may be selling away your rights under your nose. Without an impartial advocate representing you, you may not know it. And not even the brightest lawyer can tell you 100% if a deal is good for you without seeing the complete picture and understanding your individual circumstances.

I realize that this may seem complicated and frightening. But face the facts: the divorce process is serious business and you must take it seriously to ensure your welfare and the welfare of your children. A successful divorce is the foundation of a successful new life and requires making sound decisions.

You are fully capable of making these decisions. Study your options. Choose wisely and thrive.

Do You Really Need a Lawyer?

Handling your legal affairs correctly has important ramifications as you go through the divorce process and for the rest of your brand-new life. It also affects your children. Their emotional and financial well-being are at stake, and you must protect them above all considerations.

It is no secret that people *love* to hate lawyers, and you may wonder, "Do I *really* need one?" The short answer is *yes*, unless you are willing to navigate the legal minefield blindly and unassisted and endanger your welfare. I said it before, and I will say it again. At the very least, you should consult with a lawyer to understand your rights and the options available in your specific situation.

As I stated earlier, there's a lot on the line in the divorce process, and you don't want to cheat yourself or your kids of what's rightfully yours. Divorce goes way beyond terminating the marriage. Your divorce process will determine your current and future financial situation. You and your spouse will have to decide how to divide your assets *and* your debts to maintain two households with the same money that currently supports one. You may need financial support while you get yourself back on your feet—or you may have to help your spouse if you are the main breadwinner.

You will also have to make important decisions regarding your children's welfare: who has custody—legal and residential—and how the children will divide their time between the two of you. This means the school year, holidays and vacations.

Child support will be a big issue, too, and you need to make sure your children will receive proper support until they reach the age of majority. And that includes their college education!

How you go about this process will determine your quality of life, and you must handle it with care. That's why you need to understand your rights, exercise them responsibly, and pick the right lawyer to help you navigate the legal maze.

You and your spouse need to work through your differences, roll up your sleeves and collaborate to end your relationship as amicably as possible to reach a solution that makes sense.

I have a surprise for you. Contrary to what you might have heard, there are no winners in a legal battle. Legal battles are costly, both in financial and human terms. Legal fees quickly add up, and the money you need to get your life back on track or send your kids to college can easily go to paying the lawyers.

The human cost is even higher. A drawn-out battle will rob you of your peace of mind and will hold you hostage from moving on and rebuilding your life. Avoid the legal battle if you can and work with professionals who will advance your best interests, so you and your spouse can reach a workable solution.

Nobody outside your marriage understands your situation better than you do. Avoid putting life-altering decisions in the hands of a judge who does not know you or your children.

Know Your Rights

To achieve the best outcome in a divorce proceeding, you must understand your rights. Knowing your rights will help you avoid mistakes that could hurt your position, such as abandoning your home. Or it can dispel fears that are holding you back, such as the fear of losing your kids in a custody battle. And just as importantly, you don't want to walk away from what's lawfully yours.

Remember that the laws are different in every state and country, and that these laws will apply to the unique circumstances of your case.

Learn about the laws in your jurisdiction and how they affect you. If money is a problem, you can start by reaching out to your local non-profit legal services organizations. If they do not offer services at low cost, or if you don't qualify for their services, they can point you in the right direction, so you can investigate your options. Some provide downloadable brochures on their websites explaining your rights and how the divorce process works in your area. Or stop by your local courthouse and grab reliable information.

Schedule a consultation with a lawyer to better understand your individual case, what to expect and how to get the ball rolling.

Choose a Lawyer That's Right for You

Your lawyer is your first line of defense in the divorce process. He or she is the person who will stand up for you when you are losing your sanity. This is the person responsible for looking after your best interests and protecting you from yourself when you are most vulnerable. Your lawyer's job is to ensure that you get your fair share. Doesn't it make sense to select one that's a suitable match?

Picking a divorce lawyer is like picking a spouse. Your lawyer is someone you may be stuck with for a long haul, a tough ride, and splitting up is an entangled, expensive proposition. You will share with this person very personal and possibly embarrassing information, and you must feel comfortable with him or her.

Lawyers come in many flavors, and you need to choose the one who works best with you. People watch lawyers in the movies and on TV and are convinced that the best lawyer is the one with the biggest mouth. Heck, if you're going to get even with your soon-to-be-ex, you might as well hire a mean SOB to make him or her pay for all the crap you've been put through, right?

Wrong! In reality, those mean SOBs are merely grandstanding, and their effectiveness has nothing to do with how loud they scream but how well they understand the law, the judges, the case and their clients. And, in fact, those obnoxious lawyers are ineffective because they tick everybody off. The judges can't stand them, the court staff can't stand them, other lawyers don't want to work with them, and ultimately you will hate him or her, too.

A contentious SOB will also cost you a fortune, and you will be stuck footing the bill for their maniacal egos and lack of civility. You need a lawyer who will bring your case to a fair resolution as quickly and painlessly as possible. Contrary to popular belief, you are better off when the lawyers get along and have had a fine working relationship in the past.

How to Find the Right Lawyer

So how do you pick the right lawyer? By doing your research. I hear endless complaints from people—thousands of tears and dollars later—who are dissatisfied with their divorce attorneys. They believe their lawyers royally screwed them. These people did not do their homework nor chose a lawyer with care. Don't let that happen to you.

Whatever you do, do not pick a lawyer out of the Yellow Pages. Or Yelp, or the Internet. Or, God forbid, a penny saver or restaurant place mat. I cannot emphasize enough that this is a very important relationship with crucial repercussions for your life—now and in the future.

The best way to find a lawyer is through word of mouth. Ask around—especially people who have divorced recently in your area and were happy with their lawyers. And I totally mean your area.

A local lawyer is best. Why? Because a local lawyer has the home team advantage. The local lawyer knows all the players. He or she knows the *modus operandi* of the judge assigned to your case and of the lawyer representing your spouse. A local lawyer is also more likely to have worked with the same judge or lawyer before, and the lawyer's reputation in the community can be an asset in resolving your case.

In the legal field, reputation goes a long way. Professional attorneys are respected and trusted. Rude and sneaky attorneys are not. And unknown attorneys do not have the benefit of the camaraderie and professional courtesies exchanged between people who work together—or golf together—regularly.

Your personal attorney may recommend a matrimonial lawyer. Good lawyers know the other good lawyers. Similarly, nonprofit organizations are also familiar with the local attorneys who represent their clients in family law cases.

An attorney who devotes most of his or her practice to family law is a better choice, since they are more active in the field, and a busy practice keeps them informed of all the developments in family law. Whatever you do, do not hire a lawyer who does not normally practice family law, even if it's your best friend's brother or cousin. You get my drift...

Don't be deceived by the high price tag and assume that the most expensive lawyer is the best. The most experienced lawyers typically charge higher fees. But their high price tags may be tied to their expertise in handling complicated cases, with complex custody or financial issues. Your case may be more straight-forward and may not require that level of specialization. If your case is simple, please know that there are plenty of talented lawyers out there who care about helping people and charge reasonable rates. Do your homework and find them.

You may wonder, "Should I pick a male or a female lawyer?" The sex of your lawyer has no bearing on his or her ability to represent you. What truly matters is that the lawyer you select be sensitive to your needs and committed to advancing your best interests. There are many wonderful male attorneys who are sensitive and compassionate. And there are women lawyers who aren't.

It's like picking a physician. You select the best doctor whether it's a man or a woman. If you're uncomfortable sharing sensitive information with a lawyer of the opposite sex, pick the best lawyer of your same sex.

Character Traits of the Ideal Advocate

Location and legal expertise are important but not the only criteria for selecting your lawyer. To use the doctor analogy again, you want to see the doctor with the right personal qualities, not necessarily a leading expert who may lack bedside manners. Below is a short list of qualities desirable in a lawyer.

A fine lawyer:

- Listens to you and tries to understand your position, what's important to *you* and your desired outcome in the case.

- Will explain the law to you in terms you can understand instead of trying to impress you with legalese.

- Will advise you of your options and the pros and cons of each option.

- Puts your interests first. A competent lawyer is more concerned about getting a good result, rather than winning or losing, or getting rich at your expense.

- Is a skilled negotiator – at least 95% of matrimonial cases settle; your lawyer must be skilled at getting a settlement that is fair to you and gets what matters to you most.

- Is congenial and works well with you, your spouse's lawyer, the judge and other individuals involved in the case.

- Must make you feel comfortable and elicit mutual trust. Trust is essential in an attorney-client relationship. You will work together on highly sensitive matters and sharing very personal information, perhaps information that makes you feel embarrassed and you're not proud of.

- Is balanced - the best lawyers have the perfect blend of the above qualities.

There are very fine lawyers out there—if you take the time and trouble to find them. I can proudly say that I have the privilege of working with outstanding colleagues who genuinely care about their clients. And their clients love them.

And then there are the bad apples… Stay away from them. How can you tell? Here are some red flags:

- If your lawyer is condescending or talks down to you—run for the nearest door. You are the client and deserve respect.
- If the attorney talks constantly about himself or herself, you may be before a narcissist. This is *your* divorce. It is about you, not about your attorney's ego. Beware of attorneys who seem more interested in impressing you than in helping you.
- Ask how many of their cases go to trial. With most cases settling before trial, it is unusual for divorces to be decided by a judge. If the lawyer tries many of his or her cases, ask why. While many cases are client-driven, and often the clients cause their own misfortunes, you want to avoid a lawyer who will drag out your case to put his kids through college at the expense of yours.

Select Carefully—Don't Rush

Picking an attorney is not a decision that you should take lightly. It's okay to meet with more than one lawyer. Take your time and shop around until you find one who feels right, one you can trust and with whom you have a good rapport. If you have good chemistry, you will work better together. Remember, you will be a team.

It might be expensive to pay for multiple consultations. But hiring the wrong attorney will cost you more money and aggravation down the road.

Remember your friend Intuition? Ask for its guidance and trust your gut. Do your research and hire the lawyer that "feels right."

Don't Get Stuck

It's expensive to switch lawyers in the middle of a case. But if you're truly dissatisfied with your lawyer, or if you're certain that he or she is not representing you effectively, you may be better off hiring someone else. Act swiftly. Do not wait until things get too sour or too late in the case for another lawyer to step in.

Be a Good Client

Hiring the right lawyer is important, but being a good client is equally important. Be the client attorneys enjoy working with. It will make life a lot easier for you and your lawyer, and your lawyer will do a better job for you.

Lawyers sometimes complain about their clients and have pet peeves of their own. Here are some helpful tips:

- Trust is a mutual thing. Always tell your lawyer the truth and do not withhold or misrepresent information.

- Honesty is essential to effective representation and not giving your lawyer the correct information will eventually come back to bite you. Imagine if you had problems with addiction and your lawyer first heard of it as he's arguing on your behalf in a custody hearing. Disastrous!

- Don't continuously second guess your lawyer. You hired your lawyer for his or her legal expertise. Refrain from asking your friends and relatives for legal advice.

- Be reasonable. Often cases break down because clients get stuck in positions that do not serve them. Evaluate your options carefully, but do not stand in the way to a favorable resolution out of pigheadedness.

- Pay your fees.

How to Make the Most of Your Legal Fees

Legal fees quickly add up. Divorce is an expensive proposition. But you still have some control over how your money is spent.

Matrimonial lawyers typically charge in increments of six to 12 minutes (referred to as .1s and .2s) That means that they will charge you for six or 12 minutes of billable time for every thing they do for you. Depending on where you live, attorney fees could cost anywhere from $200 to $500 per hour—or more. So, that 30-second phone call, or your lawyer's time reading your one-line email, may cost you $20 to $100.

Use your attorney time wisely to avoid sticker shock:

- Don't watch your legal fees go up while you fumble. Be prepared. Get your ducks in a row. Have a list of questions and issues to discuss before your conversations with your attorney. Be straight and to the point and don't go off topic or into tangents.

- Your lawyer cannot be effective in the dark. Your lawyer cannot do his or her job without proper information. Supply the information your lawyer requests as quickly as you can. Making your lawyer hound you for it will show up in your bill.

- Do not use your lawyer as a shrink. Save your long hysterical rants for your therapist. There will be upsetting times during this process, and a mental health professional is not only cheaper, but better equipped to handle emotional matters.

- Again, be reasonable. You will be paying your lawyer to argue and drag on the case if you're stuck in an unreasonable position.

Dodge the Ugly Fight and Come Out on the Other Side

Divorce can get ugly. The movies are full of ugly divorces, like "Marriage Story." And I'm sure you've heard horror stories from your friends. But it doesn't have to be that way. And should not be that way. Divorces are public proceedings, and you will be airing your dirty laundry in public. Do your best to resolve the case without exposing your private affairs in a courtroom.

There will be trying times. Many aspects of the legal process will be out of your control, which makes divorce a frightening proposition. You can't control how a judge will decide your case or how your spouse will behave. But you can make informed decisions that will make the journey smoother and increase the odds of achieving the best possible outcome.

Most importantly, you have absolute control over your thoughts and feelings. If you start to feel upset, do your breathing exercises right away. Practice active awareness and step back before you act.

If your spouse wants to push your buttons or still has a hold on you, avoid situations that might escalate. Do not handle them alone if you feel unsafe or at a disadvantage. Politely end a conversation before it gets out of hand. You do not have to give in to reactivity—your spouse's or yours. Simply say, "Maybe we should talk about this later, when we are both calm." Hang up the phone or walk away.

In highly contentious situations, let the lawyers do the talking and get out of the way. It might cost you extra money but might save your sanity. You can choose the right team of professionals that will advance your interests when you are overwhelmed, distressed or in too much pain to think straight.

Do not take a terrible deal or renounce what is rightfully yours to avoid conflict or because you feel fearful or overwhelmed. Let your attorney deal with it. That's why attorneys make the big bucks!

On the other hand, do not cut off your nose to spite your face. Refrain from engaging in a fierce and endless battle to "make your spouse pay" for what he or she has done to you, or to get "what you think you should get" out of the divorce. Karma is ruthless, and malicious deeds to get back at your spouse will eventually come back to haunt you. The same applies to acts of fairness and kindness. They will go a long way in ironing out your differences and resolving the case expeditiously.

Keep your eyes on the prize. Do not give in to personal vendettas or thoughts of revenge. Divorce is about moving on, not about getting even.

This ordeal will end. It will be the portal to a brand-new life. Building a solid foundation is in your hands.

PART IV

POWERING UP FOR A GRACIOUS EXIT

Cruising the High Road to Divorce

Powering Up for the Journey

You now see from the earlier sections that divorce can be a complicated, bumpy life transition. Divorce is a journey, not a sprint. And to successfully arrive at your destination—freedom and fulfillment—you must prepare yourself physically and mentally, just like you would prepare for a lengthy road-trip.

Suppose you wanted to take a cross-country ride from New York to San Francisco. If you want to make it in one piece and enjoy yourself, this trip would require considerable preparation.

First, you must have a reliable vehicle. It must be in optimal condition to endure the demands of the trek. You would check the breaks, the fluids and the engine.

You'd study a roadmap and decide on the right route for you—fast or scenic—and the stops along the way. You need to check for services available, to make sure you don't run out of fuel and food.

And, just as importantly, you must make sure you are well rested and healthy—physically and emotionally—so you don't fall asleep at the wheel and crash.

You also need to ensure the journey is fun and safe. You must bring sufficient supplies—money, snacks and music CDs—and prepare for several contingencies, including inclement weather. You must be ready to handle detours and roadblocks and have the resolve to make it to the end in uncertain and ever-changing conditions.

Like a cross-country road-trip, if you're properly equipped, you can ride the road to divorce and reach your goal. And at the end you will marvel at a vast ocean of possibility, with a broader view, more wisdom, and a fresh perspective of the life you can build for yourself.

As you go through the divorce process, you may question the wisdom of your decision and consider making a U-turn to a familiar, although unhappy, situation. After all, you are leaving behind your hopes and dreams to venture into the unknown. Or you may feel disempowered by your spouse's rejection and fear you can't get through this. Therefore, powering up for the journey will improve your chances of making it to your destination healthy and unscathed.

Inner work, physical and emotional training are necessary, so you're fit to follow through with what can be a difficult and taxing process. You want to cover all bases—you don't want to wimp out because you were unprepared.

The prospect of divorce will seem overwhelming, and you may be afraid. And that is okay. You can take the emotional preparation process at your own pace, one step at a time. And you don't have to do it alone. Having the support of a counselor, family and friends will go a long way in ensuring your safe arrival.

Your life may seem bleak now; but it has brought you to this place—the only place you can start from. Get ready for a journey of healing and conscious creation. Happiness awaits you at the end of the road, because you deserve to be happy.

Building a Winning Team

Selecting Your Team Members

They say it takes a village to raise a child. I say it takes a village to make a divorce process smoother.

Studies show that social supports enhance the quality of life, reduce the psychological and physiological consequences of stress, enhance immune function and provide a buffer against adverse life events. Like divorce.

Renowned physician and best-selling author Andrew Weil, M.D., says that, "In some way, our spiritual selves resonate with others; if the interaction is positive, human connectedness is a most powerful healer, capable of neutralizing many harmful influences on the material plane."

In divorce, it is critical to have a team on your side, rooting for you and seeing you to the finish line. Putting together the right success team will make your journey more bearable and sustain you when you need encouragement and inspiration.

You must be careful in selecting the members in your support team. Not everybody has what it takes to support you. Not everybody possesses the wisdom, nor has your best interest at heart. And others will have their own agendas or infect you with their personal judgments.

If you're ambivalent about ending your marriage, some people, perhaps well-intentioned friends and relatives, will try to talk you out of divorcing. Conversely, if your spouse initiated the divorce, some friends and relatives may choose sides—not necessarily yours.

Whom to trust, then? Here's a test to determine if someone belongs on your team: Is this person going to advance your goals? Or hold you back? Try to dissuade you from doing what's right for you?

Test the grounds and share information on a "need-to-know basis." Gauge people's reactions and take it from there. Trust your intuition.

Start with a therapist and later add people to your team. A competent, caring counselor is your ultimate ally. A good therapist is someone you can trust, who won't judge you nor spill your dirt on other people you know. A good counselor will listen to you and guide you when you feel lost or discouraged. Regular meetings with a therapist will help you stay grounded and on course.

Sharing Information - The Need to Know Act

If you fear that your friends and family members would judge you or disapprove of your decision to divorce, you can continue to enjoy their love and companionship. They can support you in other ways, by loving you and spending quality time together.

You don't have to disclose any details about your marital woes or your plans until *you* feel comfortable doing so. You can wait until you feel sure they are ready to process the information and be supportive. Or you can choose to disclose such information only when you feel strong enough to handle their opposition confidently, and to stand your ground irrespective of the reactions of others.

In my case, my mother would have thwarted my plans to get out. When I hinted at problems with my husband, she countered with comments that I was too immature, that I thought life was a party and so on. She sabotaged my one attempt to leave the house by talking a friend out of giving me shelter. So after a few mishaps, I did what was best for me.

I kept my mother out of the loop until things were too far along for her to try to influence my decision. I waited until I had a court date and had signed the lease for a new apartment. When she understood that my decision was irrevocable and carefully considered, she fully supported me and took time off to help me move out of my old house into my new digs. By waiting to share the details with her, I avoided unnecessary confrontations, and protected our relationship from breaking down.

Like a press agent, you have control over what information gets out, who gets it, and the spin. You decide how to announce your departure in a way that will engender support. Choose wisely.

Who's out of the Team: Get Rid of the Chupacabras

As you assemble your support team, you intuitively know who to avoid. These are the emotional chupacabras. Like the mythical creatures that drain animals of their blood, emotional chupacabras can totally suck life out of you in a brief conversation.

Their favorite subjects—after themselves—are gossip, illness and negative news. They are hopelessly self-absorbed. They are more interested in venting their endless complaints and spewing out negative energy than in listening to you or being there for you. These people bring you down and drain your energy when you need it the most. But you don't have to put up with it.

Like the imaginary chupacabra, these people have no real power. Their grip on you is solely of your own creation. What a relief it is to know these people cannot control you! You have the power to set boundaries and choose the terms of your relationship. You have the power to say no to toxic behaviors and keep a safe distance from them.

It makes no difference if they are family or old friends. Your self-preservation takes precedence over people pleasing.

Remember, you need all your energy to heal and empower yourself.

Beat chupacabras at their own game. While in the company of a chupacabra, change the subject to something positive. Cut the conversation short. Tell them you are glad to hear from them but have only a few minutes to talk. Return their phone calls when you know they're watching their favorite shows.

If they persist, be honest and tell them you are trying to stay positive and cannot entertain negative discourse. If these people care about you and value your relationship, they will back off. If they're unable or unwilling to engage in healthy interactions, you must let them go to avoid jeopardizing your well-being.

Start to distance yourself from these individuals. If you can't completely eliminate these chupacabras from your life, set the rules of engagement. Share activities that do not involve conversation. Go see a movie together or invite them to a talk or concert. Or bring along the chatty friend who always takes over the conversation and watch in amusement as they go at it!

Whatever tactic you choose, make it your intention to protect yourself from toxic behaviors that bring you down or deplete your energy.

Expect pushback and manipulative behaviors. Chupacabras will say things like, "I thought you were my friend." Chupacabras are master manipulators and will attempt to control you. But with active awareness, their tricks won't fool you.

If you find it difficult to set boundaries to keep your life toxicity-free, embrace the situation as a learning opportunity. Explore these issues with your therapist and continue to work on them on your own until you master the art of setting healthy boundaries.

By the same token, avoid *being* a chupacabra. You may feel tempted to vent your frustrations with your family and close friends as you're going through a divorce.

I *had* a friend whose divorce led to the end of our friendship. She called screaming at all hours of the day (and night) to complain about her husband, or to dramatize every contact with the lawyers. While I tried to be supportive, her one-way conversations reeked of anger and venom and left me emotionally depleted. No amount of redirection could neutralize the tone of the conversation or calm her down. Unfortunately, this friendship could not be saved, and I had to let it go.

Don't alienate your friends. But most importantly, remember that endless complaining does not do *you* any good. Save the hardcore fury for your therapist, who is trained and gets paid to deal with it. Do not risk destroying the support systems that will carry you through divorce.

Exercise your best judgment. Engage in healthy dynamics in all of your relationships as you make your way to freedom and fulfillment.

Should You Join a Support Group?

Going through the divorce process can be rough and sometimes you may feel lonely or misunderstood. Thus, you will need all the support you can get. A support group can be an excellent source of new community—individuals experiencing similar struggles, whose company will help you mitigate feelings of loneliness and alienation. Their friendship and support could become a pillar of your new and improved life.

Ideally, a support group provides a venue to express your concerns, receive encouragement and generate ideas to move in positive directions.

But, to be useful, it has to be the right support. An inadequate support group can do more harm than good. Carefully select the support group that will advance your goals of moving on graciously and joyously.

Support groups come in many flavors. They are typically sponsored by communities of faith, divorce coaches, divorce survivors or individuals going through divorce. They can be in-person meetups or online communities such as Facebook groups and forums. DivorceCare provides highly popular and respected 13-week divorce recovery programs at thousands of locations. There is probably one near you.

Proceed with caution. Poke around and investigate the groups that appeal to you. Make sure these are groups where members exchange useful advice, encouragement and positivity. Unfortunately, some groups and forums are cesspools of toxicity and vitriol. Divorcing people often waste their energy complaining and throwing pity parties, instead of directing their attention to healing, learning their lessons and looking to the future. Don't let that happen to you!

Avoid those focused on bitching and moaning or that permit bullying and bashing exes and members of the opposite sex. Hanging around with victims and wounded warriors will leave you emotionally depleted, and possibly lead you into a misguided course of action and a harmful mental framework.

Vet each group you consider thoroughly to ensure it's the right fit. If you don't come out feeling better after a meeting or two, move on!

Even if you don't like the personality of a particular group, be on the lookout for like-minded individuals and connect before you drop out. You could provide support to one another outside of the group itself. Don't be afraid to create your own support group if you can't find one that meets your needs.

The key is to surround yourself with the kind of people and ideas that will sanely get you through the divorce process and prime you for a fresh beginning.

The Most Important Member of Your Team: You

Leaving One Best Friend for Another: Become Your Own BFF

Assembling a support team is key to ensuring your survival during divorce. But do you realize who's the most important member of your team? Yourself.

You married expecting your spouse to be your BFF. However, this best friend has let you down, and your breakup will probably leave an empty place in your heart. How to fill the void? How do you get through divorce *sans* BFF? Simple, by becoming your new best friend. You are the one and only person guaranteed to stay with you for the rest of your life. Doesn't it make sense to become your own BFF?

To strengthen this friendship, you must know this person better—the *true* you. Having been in a troubled relationship, you may have wound up with a distorted sense of self. Somehow, when you merged into the marriage, you sacrificed who you were to become a part of a couple. Ponder this... how many dreams, soul-nurturing friends and activities did you give up to make room for other friends and activities you would share with your soon-to-be ex? Did you quit school? Relinquish a promising career? Did you start spending less time with your friends and family to spend more time with your partner's friends and family instead?

How many meaningful things did you renounce because your spouse did not like them? Did you stop pursuing your interests and hobbies to make room for his or hers? Did you find yourself doing things you didn't enjoy because they were important to your mate?

While sharing and uniting with your partner may at first glance make you feel connected, at a deeper level, denying yourself the things that bring you joy ultimately erodes your sense of self. After a while, these sacrifices lead to resentment and a deep feeling of loss. And before you know it, you cease to be the person you were before you married and become an unrecognizable shell of the person you once were. And that takes a toll on your self-esteem and robs you of the joy and nurturing you received from all those things that were important to you.

That's over! It's time to take your power back and live the life that is meant for *you*. It's time to rediscover your dreams and reignite your passions. Getting reacquainted with your true self is an excellent first step to living your life authentically. Honoring the self will give you the power to deal with the issues that will arise during your divorce, the rest of your life and, if you become part of a new couple, in the future.

Rediscover your needs and desires and make honoring them a priority. Relationships are a balancing act and, to have successful relationships, you must make a commitment to respect yourself and to cultivate those relationships and activities that bring you joy. With a healthy sense of self, you will make wiser decisions that support your best interests, while respecting the needs of others.

As you follow your passions, you will discover a sense of purpose and will be guided to use your gifts to make a difference in the world. Here are some words of wisdom from social innovator and political activist Sister Stanislaus Kennedy (Sister Stan): "To be ourselves is the most wonderful thing we can be in the world. To realise the capacity we have to be ourselves is the work of a lifetime. It is the one thing we can do superbly well, and that nobody else can do."

Reflections
Did you get lost in your relationship? How?
Did your marriage "hold you back"?
In what ways?
Did it keep you away from friends and family?
Did you feel discouraged from pursuing
educational or other life-enriching activities?
Who are you outside of your relationship?

*What is your identity when you
are not with your spouse?
Are there other underlying fears—such as
failure—that kept you from pursuing your
dreams and aspirations?
What would have happened if you stood your
ground and followed your heart?
How do you think your spouse
would have responded?
How would it have affected your relationship?*

Rediscovering Your Needs and Desires

We have now established that you have somehow lost yourself as half of a couple. The next line of inquiry is—who are you— really? And most importantly, who do you want to *become*?

If you diluted your self to become a part of a couple, looking back at who you used to be is the perfect starting point before you start looking into the future. It makes sense to look back at your forsaken dreams before you start dreaming new ones. Let's look at forgotten joys before we can pursue new ones and then decide: What goes? What stays? Who goes? Who stays? Who comes in?

Let's start with an exploration of your old aspirations. Before you married, who did you want to be when you "grew up"? Were these dreams interrupted for "marital reasons"? If so, are they still your dreams or are there new and exciting things you'd like to accomplish? Is it a new career? Going back to school? Writing a book? Traveling the world?

The same applies to extracurricular activities. How did you enjoy spending your leisure time before you tied the knot? What did you give up? Would you enjoy resuming those activities? Or are there new pursuits that pique your interest? Were you an athlete who gave up on long hours of training? Or an amateur artist? A quiet contemplative who delighted in peaceful solitude? Is there something you always wanted to try, like ballroom dancing or bungee jumping, that your spouse wouldn't touch with a ten-foot pole?

And ditto with relationships. Who did you hang out with that you stopped seeing when you married? Did you replace your single friends for other married couples? Your friends and relatives for the in-laws? Do you wish to rekindle those relationships, or would you rather meet people who are more compatible with the new and improved you?

This is very exciting stuff, so don't hold back and write out your most outlandish fantasies!

Reflections - Reconnect with Your Passions
Make a list of the dreams you
had before you got married.
Do you still feel the pull? Or have they faded?
If you could be or do anything—
what would it be?
Look back at your pre-wed social life. Who were the players?
Who did you drop for lack of time or
to make room for marital obligations?
Are these people still around and is
there a mutual interest in reconnecting?
Consider calling them or looking them up on social media.
What kind of people would you like to
meet and how can you connect with them?
Get out there and meet people.
Peruse magazines and surf online to
discover fun activities you've never tried.
What activities make your heart go "thump"?
Investigate these dreams and hobbies.
Find out what it takes to pursue them
(training, equipment, locations) and write a checklist.
Take one action every day from your
checklist in at least one of these areas.

Learning to Love Number 1

Self-love: A New Way of Life

I've said it before, and I'll say it again. Lack of self-love can be a key reason that lured you into or that kept you in an unhappy marriage. Doesn't it make sense that cultivating self-love is the way out of the trap? Loving the self daily is the most effective way to build your self-esteem and get you ready for anything!

You have been through a rough patch, my friend. It is now time to take care of Number 1. We are conditioned to take care of everyone else at the expense of ourselves, especially women. We put the needs of others above our own, only to feel depleted and resentful. But once we reach that point, there's no taking care of anyone. Why do you think the safety instructions on airplanes direct adults to put on their own oxygen masks before assisting others?

Give yourself permission to indulge in nurturing practices to sustain you through the divorce process. Make a habit of caring for yourself first. It will serve you well for the rest of your life and in all of your relationships.

We are often afraid to practice self-love because we confuse it with the pariahs of selfishness, egotism, narcissism and conceit. But self-love is about honoring our needs and balancing them with our responsibilities towards others. It is making time for ourselves to refresh and rejuvenate, so we can be more effective in our everyday lives.

Practicing self-love does not require massive commitments of time and money. It can be as simple as getting into your favorite comfy clothes and reading a chapter of your newest book.

The secret is making pockets of self-indulgence daily, if only for 10 to 30 minutes, and doing something *you* find restorative. Most importantly, do not feel guilty about your "me" time. You will soon notice a difference in the way you feel and relate to your world.

Here are a few suggestions for instant relief:

- Treat yourself to a massage and melt away your stress.

- Hit the spa for a facial or mani-pedi. Or transform your home into your own spa and pamper yourself. Turn on soft music, run your tabletop water fountain, light scented candles and delight in luxurious self-care products.

- Indulge in the magic of aromatherapy and use essential oils to manage your moods. Make it a daily practice.

- Take an evening to yourself and do absolutely *nothing*. Stay at home or go somewhere you can relax and recharge the batteries. Leave the kids with another exhausted parent and offer to return the favor.

- Make a play date with your kids—or borrow someone else's kids—and have silly fun.

- Wear that special outfit that makes you feel like a million dollars and get out of the house.

For a more serious intervention, take a break from everyday tedium and treat yourself to a weekend getaway. Go by yourself or with friends. Do whatever *you* want—*no people pleasing*.

Whenever I begin to feel the signs of burnout, I check myself into a monastery for peace, quiet and healthy foods. I enjoy the time alone, curling up with an inspiring book, spending time in nature and meeting spiritual people. I emerge refreshed, ready to face the challenges of life with poise and grace.

When you take care of yourself, you send a signal to the world—and to yourself—that you are deserving and receptive to the blessings of life. Self-care is a conduit for more abundance and joy. Make a commitment to honor your desires and allow the magic of self-love to revolutionize your life.

For a deep life-changing experience, devote a year to loving yourself. Check out the book *The Art of Extreme Self-Care: Transform Your Life One Month at a Time* by Cheryl Richardson, also available as an online course on Hay House. It contains a wealth of information, exercises and resources to help you upgrade yourself and live more fully.

Nurturing Your Spirit

Staying Inspired

With all the changes, uncertainty and upheaval in your life, at times you will feel down and discouraged. Now more than ever you will need to keep your spirits high and your soul nourished. An inspired life knows no bounds. It's immune from limitation. It can weather anything. Inspiration is the antidote to fear.

Stay inspired and keep your outlook positive, regardless of your circumstances. If you focus on the negative, you won't be able to see the way out of your problems. I am not suggesting you go into denial and numb yourself. However, elevating your mood promotes introspection, stimulates problem solving and dissolves negativity. The key is to keep yourself uplifted and to identify ways to bounce back when you get knocked down.

Fortunately, there are sources of inspiration everywhere, many of them free. So, experiment with those that work for you and align with your personal values. Below is my list of favorites.

Tap into the Wealth of Inspirational Materials
Daily Inspirational Readings

Start your day on a top note with a jolt of inspiration. I am a fan of reading morning meditations and won't leave the house without doing them first. I have been reading *The Daily Word* since I was in junior high school. Most recently, I discovered *Angel Wisdom: 365 Meditations and Insights from the Heavens*, by Terry Lynn Taylor and Mary Beth Crain, and was introduced to *Gardening the Soul: Mindful Thoughts and Meditations for Every Day of the Year*, by Sister Stan. These publications infuse me with the grace I need to face every day with poise and faith.

There are infinite choices, from religious to secular. You will never run out of options, from hardcover books to apps you can download to your phone or tablet, to calendars of inspirational quotes. Go to your local bookstore and peruse the shelves. Or browse online until you find an inspirational reading that hits the spot, so you can always have encouragement at your fingertips.

So Many Teachers, So Little Time

Where were all these teachers when I was going through my divorce? Luckily for you, these days you can find amazing teachers who can revolutionize your world and bless you with their wisdom and contagious joy and enthusiasm. I keep finding teachers almost daily, and a lifetime is not enough to get to know them all!

There is outstanding work on every topic imaginable, from relationships to spirituality, positive thinking, law of attraction and success—you name it! With the magic of the Internet, and YouTube in particular, you can read about and listen to all these gifted individuals and get pumped up in a heartbeat.

I have been enjoying the books from Jack Canfield and Mark Victor Hansen's *Chicken Soup for the Soul* series since they first came out and have studied many other personal development teachers. I have listed some of them on the Resources page at the end of this book.

Once you start researching teachers, you will be surprised by how many more will come to your awareness, some famous, some lesser known. As you open your heart to guidance, you will discover the teacher who is perfect for your specific need every time. As the old saying goes, "When the student is ready, the teacher appears."

You can find teachers to uplift you in every imaginable situation. Keep looking until you discover the one(s) that resonate with *you* and whose delivery styles you enjoy. While my husband is jazzed by Tony Robbins' success message and high energy personality, I prefer spiritual, soothing materials, like those by the late Wayne Dyer and Louise Hay.

Listen to audiobooks, watch videos and check out the teachers' websites. From old classics like Earl Nightingale,

Joseph Murphy and Napoleon Hill to the present-day luminaries, like Don Miguel Ruiz, you will find someone to deliver the comfort and fortitude you need right now.

Spiritual Homecoming - for the People of Faith

Regardless of your faith—Buddhism, Christianity, Hinduism, Islam or Judaism—connecting or reconnecting with your God can provide you with sustenance and comfort as you go through divorce. My faith was my bastion as I endured years of misery in my marriage and as I braved the unknown as a newly single young woman. I was supported by loving clergy, and that made all the difference.

But unfortunately, religion can also bring hardship and stress, as I stated earlier. Some religions condemn and reject divorced individuals. Understandably, many of them feel like second-class citizens and stay away from their faith altogether, when they need it the most. Thankfully, those mindsets are changing, though not fast enough for the people involved.

Regardless of your religion's dogma, don't let divorce build a barrier between you and your God. Even if your religion frowns on divorce, God will still be there for you. Turn to God in your heart, where God *is*, and do not give up on the one relationship that matters the most.

While I can't imagine survival without God's help, I know that not everybody shares my belief system. And I totally respect their right to their views.

If you are not a believer, investigate other inspirational resources, like The Sedona Method or the works of Elizabeth Gilbert, Lisa Nichols and Brene Brown. They will uplift you without the religiosity that puts many people off. But whatever you do, seek stillness, and keep your spirit nourished and strong.

Music

Music is hands down the ultimate antidote to a miserable mood. Science has corroborated the beneficial effects of music on your health and stress levels. Listening to music releases dopamine, a chemical in your brain with a key role in setting good moods.

Music has the power to soothe and relax you when you're tense or anxious. It lifts your spirits and infuses you with courage when you're feeling weak. It also boosts your immune system and creativity.

How can anyone stay down after listening to Pharrell Williams' song "Happy"? Can you listen to Queen's classic "We Are the Champions" and not feel uplifted? Could you possibly hang on to stress while listening to Mozart? Music works miracles with little effort on your part.

Let music do your bidding. Take out your old CDs, look up new artists and experiment with different kinds of music. Pay attention to their effects on your mood. You must have your favorites. Make a playlist to dissolve obstacles to a serene and joyful mood. Download the most effective tunes to your phone or tablet, so you can access them quickly in case of emergency, to shift your mood on the spot.

Here's a short list of musical fortifiers to cheer you up when you need a lift:

- Amy Winehouse - "Tears Dry on their Own"
- Beyonce - "Best Thing I Never Had"
- Ariana Grande - "Break Free"
- Destiny's Child - "I'm a Survivor"
- Gloria Gaynor - "I Will Survive"
- Justin Timberlake - "Cry Me a River"
- Tubthumping - "I Get Knocked Down"

Reflections
What inspires you?
What elevates your mood?
Make a list and practice three
things from the list daily.
Keep a list of your favorites in your wallet, so
you can go through them whenever
you need a pick-me-up.

Life-transforming Practices

Learn to view your marital strife as a training ground for a more awakened living. This is the perfect time to redesign your life and play with new life-affirming techniques to support you during the divorce process and beyond. Rejoice in the discovery process. Embrace those ideas that help you the most or alternate them according to your mood and situation.

Daily Rituals

Daily self-love rituals will go a long way in strengthening you and helping you maintain your poise and sanity whether you revive or exit your relationship. Rituals provide stability amid chaos and changing circumstances. And making sacred time for yourself everyday signals to your subconscious mind that you're important and valuable.

I came to understand the value of ritual when my mother had two nearly fatal heart attacks and was in critical condition. What drove it home for me was caring for my mother at the hospital. Her odds of survival were slim, and my dad and I were the only ones who knew it. I felt powerless and alone.

I gained a sense of stability and peace from doing the same routine every morning: the bath, feeding her breakfast, reading the Psalms. This routine infused me with a sense of control in a situation full of uncertainty. It kept me grounded in the midst of fear and isolation.

From that moment on I have sworn by the power of ritual to tolerate the unbearable and rise above it. Rituals are also a powerful mechanism for cultivating self-love.

The experts agree. In their video program *You Can Trust Your Life*, Louise Hay and Cheryl Richardson emphasize the importance of daily rituals as a vehicle to promote self-love and self-acceptance.

Start each day on the right track. Make a commitment to yourself. Develop inviolable daily rituals that make you feel special. They can be as simple as a quiet cup of coffee or your favorite tea. Savor your beverage in a fine china cup or a funny mug. Treat yourself to a healthy smoothie served in a fancy tall glass and feel like you're on vacation in the Caribbean.

Read the paper or your daily devotionals. Squeeze in an invigorating workout that is fun. Spend some time meditating or listening to uplifting music. Devote a few minutes to say affirmations that set an upbeat tone for the day. Get up a little earlier, so you have enough time to complete your routine without feeling rushed.

Keep in mind that rituals are not just for the mornings. Create rituals to help you decompress at the end of the day, when you come home from work and before going to sleep.

Set time aside to relax and switch gears and leave behind the baggage of the day. I will share more relaxing evening routines in a subsequent chapter.

The key to fruitful "ritualing" is to make it your own. Engage in activities that make *you* feel joyous. This is not the time to do the things you "should," like a workout you hate, paying bills or reconciling your bank account. Delight in every minute of your rituals without guilt and witness your feelings of well-being soar.

Reflections
Do you have any uplifting
routines in your life?
How do they affect your mood? Your day?
What routines can you incorporate
in your life to ground you and center you?

Gratitude

Living in a state of gratitude is the "not-so-secret" of joyful living. Gratitude is the single, most effective practice you can add to your repertoire. Be grateful for everything in your life, and you will begin to see your joy levels surge exponentially. Gratitude will make you feel rich.

Spiritual and inspirational teachers alike deem gratitude an essential practice in personal evolution. Without a doubt, gratitude is the conduit for bringing more of what you desire into your life. When you have feelings of gratitude, you are telling your subconscious mind that you are blessed and abundant, and therefore deserving of attracting even more blessings.

Think about this… When you're ungrateful for what you have, you are fixating on lack and limitation. When you think you do not have enough, you are defining yourself as an impoverished person.

With your vision focused on scarcity, you are unlikely to notice the good things around you. You will miss the new job posting. You will repel the person who could introduce you to that important contact. The million-dollar idea will not occur to you. Simply put, you will not attract or notice those opportunities that could turn your life around.

As an unhappily married soul, you must wonder, "What can I be grateful about? My life stinks!"

Perhaps your life stinks right now. But your life will not smell like roses if you keep your head stuck in the toilet.

Grab your journal and start feeling grateful. Write a list of 25 things you are grateful for. Can't think of anything? Ponder this:

- You can vote.
- You can go to school.
- You can speak your mind.
- You have running water and indoor plumbing.

- You can practice a profession of your choice.
- You can practice the religion of your choice or no religion at all.
- You got to pick that spouse that is making you crazy.

People living in other countries cannot. As I think about our brothers and sisters in restrictive regimes and war-torn countries, I can't help but feel blessed for living in the United States, with all its flaws and petty annoyances. You can find many other reasons to feel lucky and happy. They are everywhere.

Practicing gratitude is free and easy and will do wonders for your mood. It is as simple as noticing everything that comes to your attention.

You can begin when you wake up in the morning, feeling grateful for your bed, your pillow, a warm blanket and a good night's sleep.

Appreciate the simple things that you normally take for granted, like soap, a shower with hot water and good water pressure. By the time you leave your house and face the outside world, you've had dozens of things to be grateful for.

And don't stop there! Continue noticing everything. Rejoice in flowing traffic. Say a heartfelt thank you to all the people who perform a service for you, like the barista who always gets your coffee just right. They will respond to your appreciation and keep the good karma going.

You can even be thankful for the seemingly negative things that happen to you, because they often bring fresh new blessings and powerful lessons that transform your existence.

Oprah Winfrey urges her followers to keep a gratitude journal and to list in it every night five events of the day they are grateful for. Once you incorporate gratitude into your every experience, you will notice happy synchronicities happening non-stop. At first, they may be little things, what is often referred to as "the green lights and the parking spaces." But after a while, bigger miracles will occur more frequently. You will receive countless things to be thankful for.

Gratitude has a higher return on your investment than any other practice you can take up. Start counting your blessings—now!

Meditation

We have already discussed the benefits of meditation to help you clear your mind and tap into your intuition for guidance. In a culture that worships multitasking, meditation may seem like a waste of time, and I have already given you a lot of homework. Yet, this is important because maintaining a formal daily practice improves your overall well-being. Like gratitude, when embraced as a way of life, meditation will pay off handsome rewards.

And don't take it from me. The perks of meditation have been widely researched. Studies show that meditation has many physical and emotional benefits. Meditation is linked to reduced stress levels, relief from depression and anxiety, and enhanced concentration and decision-making skills. Health benefits include lower blood pressure, improved sleep, better management of chronic pain and heart disease and many others. So don't quit now. Keep meditating for your health and your sanity.

Journaling

Besides completing the writing exercises in the Reflections sections throughout this book, I highly recommend writing in a journal to help you sort out your feelings and gain clarity. Journaling is the ultimate navigational tool in your journey of self-discovery and mastery. It helps you understand where you are in life, where you want to be, and chart how you will get there.

Journaling provides a unique opportunity to examine where you've been and the person you used to be. It helps you connect the dots. A journal is a silent witness to the transformation into the person you are becoming. Your journal is a roadmap to your goals and dreams and the historian of your life journey.

Journaling has been instrumental in my personal evolution. Inspired by Little Lulu, I started journaling when I was eight years old in a little Mickey Mouse diary someone brought me from Disney World.

I have since written volumes of journals at every stage in my life. Reading them back has reconnected me to the frightened child, the rejected adolescent, the hopeful young adult, and the grown woman who has faced and overcome a multitude of challenges in health, career and marriage.

Reading old journals has helped me understand myself and my relationships and echoed the voices that got me into trouble. Reading old journals has armed me with the sense of invincibility that comes with surmounting trials and tribulations and overcoming pain and defeat. My journals have been the friends that cheer me on, shouting, "You got through all this and you can get through anything." Journaling can do the same for you.

Journaling is empowering. Journaling is liberating. It is one area in your life where you have total control, where there are no rules or *you* make the rules, if you so choose. Your journal is your own. You can write what you want, how you want. It is the place where you unload your deepest secrets and your sacred aspirations, dreams and hopes. There's no need to hold back, and you can tell it like it is. Nobody is listening, and nobody will judge you.

As you reflect on your marriage, contemplate whether to stay or leave, or plot your next steps as you go through divorce, putting your thoughts on paper will bring you clarity, release powerful emotions and help you articulate your future moves.

Not sure what to write? *Anything.* Here are a few suggestions:
- The events of the day.
- Your innermost thoughts and feelings.
- Things you are grateful for.
- Your hopes, dreams and aspirations.
- Your goals and completion timelines.
- Things that make you happy.

- Things you want to accomplish and places you wish to visit.

The beauty of the journal is that you can look back at earlier entries and reflect on your progress. How have you grown? What challenges have you overcome? What have you learned from them?

You can congratulate yourself on your triumphs and identify those areas you still need to work on. Your journal is a friend who reflects your beauty back to you and honestly tells you when you're on the wrong track.

You can write in a stream-of-consciousness format. Or your journal can be poetic, prose or a combination of styles. You can vent the vilest thoughts you dare not say out loud or allow yourself to be vulnerable. It can contain an unsent letter to your spouse expressing your thoughts and feelings or an unsent letter to any other person who has touched your life in a good or a bad way.

To be effective, journaling must be uncensored, unfiltered and from the heart. If you are concerned about privacy and fear that someone—your spouse in particular—will read your journal, take precautionary measures. Keep it in a place where he or she won't have access to it. If you're married to someone as nosey as my ex-husband, take advantage of online journaling apps, which offer a variety of features to protect your privacy. Choose the one that's right for you.

For added inspiration, buy an attractive journal that you enjoy looking at. Write with a fancy pen or with ink in bright, fun colors. Jazz it up with stickers. Select a writing place where you feel calm and at ease and make journaling your therapy.

While 20 minutes a day is desirable, do not limit yourself to this amount of time nor skip journaling for lack of time. At least scribble a paragraph saying you're too tired, overwhelmed or too busy to write more. A brief entry will record your state of mind and help you understand yourself and your moods.

Consistency is the key. Make it a date with yourself every day. Make it part of your "me" routine and watch your inner wisdom unfold and guide you. For a more profound experience to connect with your life, spur creativity and heighten your spiritual and professional development, check out the Progoff Intensive Journal Program for Self-Development.

Affirmations: Food for the Spirit

Repeating affirmations is a quick and easy way to help you manifest your fondest desires. Affirmations have been around for a long time and are recommended by countless self-help gurus.

There is nothing mysterious or "woo woo" about affirmations. Simply put, every thought you think and every word you speak is an affirmation. It is a message you send out to the world—and to yourself. Affirmations mirror your feelings inside and what appears in your outer world. Accordingly, the conscious use of affirmations is a powerful way to create your life intentionally.

Every time you utter the words "I am," you are declaring something about yourself that the world and your subconscious mind will accept as true and reflect back to you. When you say, "I'm undesirable," or "I am unlovable," you are stating an affirmation that devalues you and repels the love that could be yours.

By contrast, when you say to yourself, "I can do this," or "I am the master of every situation," you boost your confidence and feelings of well-being, and you feel empowered to create a life where you are in control.

You can use affirmations to dissolve the obstacles that hold you back and purposely use positive affirmations to create, within and without you, a positive tone that will resonate in your outer world. Retrain your brain to replace negative thoughts, words and feelings with thoughts, words and feelings of harmony, success and possibility. When you infuse them with emotion, affirmations become even more powerful and speed up the creative process.

Allow the power of this free tool to assist you in creating the life of your dreams. You can create affirmations for every area of your life, such as personal empowerment, relationships, prosperity or health.

Set some special time aside each day to say your affirmations. Repeating affirmations is most useful when you get up in the morning, to set a happy vibe for the day, and at night, before you fall asleep, to place your order with your subconscious mind to bring you a wonderful tomorrow.

Place written affirmations where you can see them as constant reminders of your intentions. On the mirror, your desk, your computer, your screen savers—everywhere. Repeat them over and over throughout the day, especially as you face challenges and roadblocks.

Surround Yourself with Beauty

One of the easiest ways to keep your spirits up is to surround yourself with beauty. Social innovator and political activist Sister Stanislaus Kennedy (Sister Stan) says that, "*The only gift that is greater than beauty is our awareness of it.*" She writes, "*Nature opens windows of wonder to us daily, but it is up to us to notice the windows and to look through them. If we do that, we live each day against a collage of wonder.*"

What a gift it is to experience life with a sense of wonder! When you make it your intention to see beauty everywhere, you will inevitably find it. And your life will be transformed. Why? Because beauty stimulates the brain to produce the chemicals that make us feel good.

According to Dr. David R. Hawkins, beauty has a physical influence on the brain, proliferating neurons and energizing the side of the brain that puts out endorphins—our feel-good chemicals. Dr. Hawkins recommended that parents expose their children to beauty—nature, art, classical music and literature—to facilitate their spiritual evolution.

But you don't have to be a child nor have a doctoral degree to understand or benefit from the magic of beauty. Beauty is everywhere. Train yourself to find beauty in everything you encounter—the sunflower growing in a crack on the pavement, a magnificent sunset, children at play—and intentionally incorporate it into your life.

Spend Time in Nature

As Sister Stan correctly points out, nature is the obvious portal to beauty and wonder. Think about it. Nature is the ultimate source of creation and healing. Notice how nature continuously creates and renews itself—on a daily basis as well as when there is a natural disaster. That same power to heal can restore your body and soul.

The benefits of spending time in nature have been extensively studied and documented. Research shows that spending time in nature has positive effects on blood pressure, cholesterol, outlook on life, stress reduction and mental health, among others.

Personally, nature has been a source of sustenance and inspiration. I've had many aha moments in nature. Walking through the forests of New Zealand, I found myself full of insights and ideas for this book.

Uplift your spirits! Spend time in nature every day, even if it's just a brief walk in the park. Take your shoes off and feel the sensations of your feet on the grass, soil or sand! Meditate outdoors and feel the wisdom of nature infuse you.

It is just as easy to take nature home with you and make it a part of your daily experience. Hang a bird feeder outside your window where you can enjoy the birds. Plant a garden. It can be as simple as a small container on your porch or yard.

Do you live in a city or a tiny apartment? No problem. Nature can come with you there, too! If space is in short supply, grow fresh herbs in pots on your windowsill. They are perfect for cooking, and you will be participating in the mystery of creation.

Do you suffer from a black thumb? No excuses. Buy yourself flowers or a blooming plant and feel your mood perk up!

A rock collection is another option to bring the power of nature into your intimate surroundings. You can pick up interesting stones you find in your nature escapades or purchase stones at specialty stores. Stones possess positive energy and can be a constant reminder of the life-affirming effects nature can contribute to your life. A fountain is yet another possibility to help you melt your stress away with the soothing sounds of the rushing water.

The bottom line is that beauty offers an unlimited supply of joy. There's no place where beauty is absent—especially in natural surroundings. If you're open to seeing it, it is free and yours for the taking. Use it to sustain you as you go through your divorce journey and beyond. And every day you will live your life against a collage of wonder.

Embracing Healthy Habits

You are beginning your life anew. This an excellent time to start fresh and adopt new habits to keep you mentally and physically well and face the stress of marital unhappiness with courage and confidence.

The key components of physical health are nutrition, exercise and rest. Divorce presents a marvelous opportunity to take better care of your health, so you can endure the rigors of the divorce process.

Now is the time to take care of your mind, body and spirit. As a precaution, consult with your doctor or another health professional before trying out any new health regimes, to make sure they are right for you.

Eat Well

You may feel tempted to eat your heart out and console your broken heart with a pint of Ben and Jerry's or a whole Pepperidge Farm cake. But eating healthy is an antidote to the blues. Avoid the guilt that inevitably follows giving in to a crazy craving. All your problems will still be there, besides damaging your body and mind. Why? Poor nutrition contributes to stress, exhaustion, and impairs your capacity to work. Over time, poor nutrition increases your risk of developing a variety of health problems.

Poor eating habits include over-eating, not supplying your body with sufficient healthy foods, or consuming the wrong foods, so you don't get enough nutrients or get too much of those ingredients that are bad for you.

The good news is that eating well is simpler than you think and, once you adopt healthy eating habits, simply delicious. Eating healthy is an investment that will pay off in the way you look and feel. Eating a nutritious diet improves your feelings of well-being, increases your energy levels and improves your overall health. Eating healthy boosts your ability to fight off and recover from illness. It reduces the risk of some diseases, including high blood pressure and cholesterol, heart disease, diabetes, stroke and some types of cancer, among others.

Proper nutrition doesn't mean dieting or starving yourself, but instead means eating a balanced diet that includes the right amount of lean proteins, carbs and fats. With such a variety of food products out there, tricky advertising and incomprehensible labels, it's hard to figure out what's best for you. And the plethora of diets that promise fast weight loss only add to the confusion.

Learn from the experts. Talk to your doctor or a nutritionist and devise the right plan to keep you in optimal health. Your insurance plan may cover nutritional guidance, and even some supermarkets offer free consultations with nutritionists. A professional can help you design an eating plan that is just right for your health, age and physical activity levels.

Select foods that help you manage your physical ailments and boost your mood. Set up an appointment to get started on the plan that will keep you healthy and trim. You will feel and look your best. What are you waiting for? Get started now!

Get Your Daily ZZZs

Marital miseries will lead to sleepless nights. All the more reason to make it your intention to get enough sleep. Sleep is the sacred time when your body restores itself. This is when tissue growth and repair occur, your energy is replenished, and hormones are released. It comes as no surprise that sleep is critical to your well-being.

Sleep is essential for learning and a healthy memory, regulating your metabolism and weight, maintaining a healthy mood and protecting your cardiovascular health. Sleep is also important to safety, as sleep loss contributes to falling asleep when you need to be alert, leading to accidents and making mistakes.

How do you know if you're getting enough sleep? Individual sleep needs vary, but most adults need an average of six to 10 hours per night. If you find yourself tired or falling asleep in the middle of the day or while watching TV, chances are you're not sleeping long enough.

Here are some tips from the American Sleep Association for getting a good night's sleep:

- Go to bed at the same time every night, plus or minus 30 minutes.
- Keep your bedroom dark—turn off all lights and close your blinds.
- Keep your bedroom cool—70 degrees is the ideal temperature.
- Avoid caffeine and alcohol five hours before bed.
- Avoid reading and watching TV in bed.
- Avoid activities associated with being awake.
- Have a relaxing ritual, like meditation or listening to soft music.

To this excellent advice I will add incorporating inspirational activities before bed. My personal favorites include visualization and saying affirmations before hitting the pillow. Also, take a few minutes to review your day and express gratitude for the blessings received and the lessons learned—make a quick entry in your journal for added impact.

The bonus of these simple life-affirming steps is that they enhance your dream life and create the life of your dreams. Use your pre-bed minutes every night to program your subconscious mind to create the perfect tomorrow.

Finally, resist the temptation to rely on sleeping aids for your nightly rest. Most sleep-inducing drugs are addicting and can wreak havoc on your sleeping hygiene. You may ultimately be unable to fall and stay asleep on your own. If you practice the above steps and you still find yourself sleep deprived, talk to your doctor at once and get professional help.

Get Moving

Want to feel happier and healthier? Then get your butt off the couch! You may feel down and not motivated to move but do it anyway. You will feel much better after a good sweat.

We are all familiar with the physical benefits of exercise. Exercise helps control your weight, strengthens your muscles and bones, and reduces your risk of developing nasty conditions like type 2 diabetes, heart disease and some forms of cancer.

But the benefits of exercise aren't only physical. According to the Association for Applied Sport Psychology (AASP), exercising increases your feelings of energy, improves your mood, self-esteem and body image. It also reduces stress, helps you cope with stress and decreases symptoms of depression.

Once you experience these psychological benefits, you will become motivated to continue exercising to keep the good feelings coming. How much exercise do you need to produce those effects? Not a lot.

The AASP says that even a brief walk at low intensity can improve mood and increase energy. As little as 10 minutes of aerobic exercise can have a positive effect. For long-term benefits, exercise three times a week for 30 minutes per session at a moderate intensity. However, keep in mind that programs longer than 10 weeks work best for reducing symptoms of depression.

You may be thinking, "But exercise is so boring! And hard!" We've all heard that odious expression, "No pain, no gain!" Exercise doesn't have to be hard. It can be fun and even enhance your social life. Take a class or join a club or gym to escape the house and meet people.

Not a gym person? Neither am I! Then start walking! Research showed that a brisk 30-minute walk three times a week was more effective in reducing depression symptoms than leading depression drugs. Walkers were also less likely to have a recurrence of depression. And take your walk in nature for even more benefits to your physical and mental health! Or bring your puppy along!

The key is doing something that's fun *to you*, so you will stick with it. Play with a kid. Play like a kid. Enlist a fitness buddy to make your workouts more enjoyable and to keep each other accountable for reaching your fitness goals.

My favorite: take a dance class to express your creativity and experience joy. I take private Flamenco dance lessons because Flamenco makes me feel beautiful, stomping helps me release negative emotions, and I love spending time with my teacher, Lisa Botalico. This enjoyable workout doubles as laugh therapy, as we have outrageous fun.

You can try other forms of dance exercise, whether it's Zumba, ballroom dancing or capoeira, Brazil's unique blend of music, martial arts and dance. Shake your bon bon!

Crazy schedule? You can still find time for fitness. With such a variety of videos to choose from, many available online, lots of them free, and quite a few for 10 minutes or less, you have no reasons to not get moving.

If you're uneasy about exercising for fear of getting hurt, there's good news. According to the Centers for Disease Control and Prevention (CDC), the health benefits of physical activity far outweigh the risks of getting hurt. Moderate-intensity aerobic activity, like brisk walking, is generally safe for most people. The CDC recommends starting slowly and gradually increasing your level of activity. However, if you have a chronic health condition like arthritis, diabetes, or heart disease, talk with your doctor first to find out if your condition in any way limits your ability to be active. Then, work with your doctor to come up with a physical activity plan that matches your abilities.

If your condition stops you from meeting their minimum Guidelines, try to do as much as you can. The key is not being inactive. Even 60 minutes a week of moderate-intensity aerobic activity is good for you. Exercise will also help you sleep better. Dare to try something new and exciting and see yourself growing in confidence and strength.

Breathe!

We were born programmed to breathe without having instruction, so we take breathing for granted without giving it any thought. But doing breathing exercises can do you a world of good and help you cope with the anxiety and stress of relationship strife.

Renowned physician and best-selling author Andrew Weil, M.D., states that, if he had to limit his advice on healthier living to just one tip, it would be learning how to breathe correctly. Dr. Weil has been helping patients restore their health over two decades, and I consider his book, *Spontaneous Healing: How to Discover and Enhance Your Body's Natural Ability to Maintain and Heal Itself*, instrumental in managing my debilitating autoimmune disorders.

In this book, Dr. Weil recommends practicing breathing exercises for relaxation and optimum health. His 4-7-8 breathing exercise is very simple and quick, requires no special equipment, and you can practice it anywhere, anytime.

You can do this exercise in any position, but Dr. Weil recommends sitting with your back straight while you learn the technique. Here's how:

- Put the tip of your tongue against the ridge of tissue just behind your upper front teeth and keep it there through the entire exercise.
- Begin by exhaling completely through your mouth around your tongue, making a whoosh sound. If you find it difficult to exhale with your tongue in place, try pursing your lips until you get the hang of it.
- Close your mouth and inhale quietly through your nose to a count of four.
- Hold your breath for a count of seven.

- Exhale completely through your mouth, making a whoosh sound to a count of eight.
- This routine is considered one breath. Inhale again and repeat the cycle three more times for a total of four breaths.

That's it! Yet, this simple breathing exercise is a natural tranquilizer for the nervous system and becomes more powerful with repetition and practice. Do the 4-7-8 exercise at least two times a day. You cannot do it too frequently, but start slowly, with four or less breaths per practice during the first month. As you progress, you can later increase to eight breaths twice a day. Please note that speed is not important when doing this exercise. The key is keeping the ratio of 4-7-8 for inhalation, hold and exhalation.

As you master this technique with daily practice, you will reap a variety of health benefits. Dr. Weil considers this exercise a tonic for the nervous system. It also helps digestive problems, lowers high blood pressure and combats anxiety and insomnia.

Try it whenever you start to feel anxious or stressed. As you become upset, start breathing before you react.

For more breathing exercises and other health tips, visit Dr. Weil's website, and check out his book and audio course *Breathing: The Master Key to Self-Healing*.

Crushing Stress Before It Crushes You

There's no sugarcoating it. Divorce is stressful. With all the uncertainty and change inherent in divorce, you will likely feel uneasy, worry about your future and experience pressure.

Pulling your hair out yet? Please don't. There's much you can do to neutralize the grip stress has over you and, paradoxically, turn it into your ally. Stress is an indicator of areas where you need change and an invitation to rise to the occasion, so you can turn obstacles into opportunities.

Dr. Wayne Dyer said there is no such thing as stress. After all, you cannot see or measure stress. Stress is something you feel inside that will show up on the outside as dis-ease, making mistakes and having accidents.

So why surrender to a non-existent force?

As you experience these oppressive feelings, you probably can't fathom how much control you have over your experience. But you do.

Here's some food for thought... Notice how different people handle themselves in stressful situations. Under similar circumstances, some people manage, others break down while others thrive.

Evidently, stress has more to do with how you react to a situation than with the situation itself. Simply put, stress is *your response* to what's going on around you.

So the cure for stress, naturally, lies within.

To improve your response, you must first identify your stress triggers, analyze your response, and implement alternate responses that may better serve you.

As you go through the inquiries outlined below, you may realize that many of your fears and worries are unfounded. Or you may realize that you can successfully take them on.

Here's my three-step strategy to defeat stress. Ask yourself:

- "What am I stressed about?"
- "How does stress show up in my body?"
- "What I am telling myself when I feel stressed out?"

Let's put it into practice with some common scenarios.

What's Stressing You Out?

Feelings of stress may have various origins, and you must recognize them before you can dissolve them. Do you have too much on your plate? Are you catastrophizing, letting uncertainty and fear of the unknown get the best of you? Are you worried about your finances? Are you overwhelmed by undertakings beyond your comfort zone or outside of your area of expertise? Are you concerned about your relationships with your family and friends and how divorce will affect them?

Once you realize what's upsetting you, you can implement a plan of action to bring relief.

How Do You Know You're Stressed Out? Find the Stress in Your Body

Pay attention to your physical sensations when you are stressed out. Notice when they first appear. What thought or situation preceded that sensation? Do you feel a lump in your throat when the phone rings and the caller id shows the phone number of your lawyer or soon-to-be-ex? Does your stomach churn before child visitation exchanges? Do you get a headache every time a bill arrives in the mail?

Implementing Coping Strategies

Once you identify the causes of your stress, you can develop strategies to solve what troubles you. Here are some solution-oriented techniques to help you deal with a few stressful scenarios common to the divorce universe.

If You're Overextended, Get Help!

Are you biting off more than you can chew? If so, this isn't the time to be a hero. This is the time to take care of yourself and allow others to care for you.

I know that for many of us it feels unnatural to ask for help. You may think you *should* do it all. Or you fear that people will say "No" to your requests.

Get over it! Seek the help you need to get through this. Ask friends and family; or hire someone—perhaps a student strapped for cash. If you are strapped for cash, barter favors with another overwhelmed soul who may welcome the help and the mutual support.

Don't take on more than you can humanly do. Make a list of your commitments and calculate how much time they sap out of your life. Identify which ones are strictly necessary and which are not. Which can you delegate? Which can you let go?

If you have a propensity to bite more than you can chew, please, do not take another bite before you choke! Learn to say "No." Don't be shy about turning down additional commitments. You may feel ashamed to say no out of fear of being disliked. But this is not the time to put others above self. Your survival comes first. It is instinctual to want to help others, but you must acknowledge and honor your limits.

If you grew up with the belief that it is unkind to say "No," remember that you don't have to be mean to say "No." You can simply say, "I would love to help you, but this is not a good time. I will be happy to help when things fall into place." If people can't accept that, they are not your friends and you should feel no remorse for not giving in to their demands.

If You're Over Your Head

If you're facing issues outside of your area of expertise, seek professional help. Reach out to friends and relatives with knowledge in those areas. Or ask around your community of faith for referrals.

Or educate yourself and learn to handle these matters confidently. Divorce may present you with an amazing opportunity to learn something new and enhance your skill set. I know people who started new careers because they ended up enjoying things they were forced to learn as a result of their divorce.

Research online for resources, take a course, or pay a visit to your local library. You may find nonprofit organizations that can help or point you in the right direction.

The key is to *do something,* instead of giving in to despondency. Take a baby step and then another.

Life unfolds one moment at a time. Taking action will enhance your feelings of competency and empower you to face challenges with confidence.

Don't Let Your Spouse Drag You to Hell

Your spouse's behavior may be a prime source of stress throughout the divorce process. But understand that you cannot control or change others. You can only control yourself. Your soon-to-be-ex is responsible for his or her actions, and you are only responsible for your own.

How you react to your ex's behavior is your responsibility. Do not relinquish control of your feelings. *You* are in command.

A friend of mine found himself in the middle of a hideous divorce. His wife was a vicious *agent provocateur* who frequently and needlessly called to instigate conflict. So, he decided not to engage her, and he had the lawyers handle her calls. Instead, he harnessed his energy towards generating prosperity after divorce and has rebuilt his life beautifully.

Notice when your ex is pushing your buttons. Make a commitment to remain undisturbed. Witness his or her behaviors with curiosity without getting entangled into the provocations. Take a step back and respond instead of reacting on autopilot.

Then, reward yourself every time you keep your cool and come out unscathed.

Remind yourself that this will be over and that you won't be married to this person anymore. *And feel grateful for that.*

If you have children together, remember that your ex will remain in your life. *You* get to decide what role he or she will play in it. So, focus on your relationship with the children and on keeping it strong.

Tap into Your Support Systems

I cannot overemphasize the importance of support systems. Divorce will lead to feelings of isolation, and I devoted an entire chapter to this topic. Go back and read it. Surround yourself with upbeat people who will lift your spirits. Especially people who have been through divorce themselves and are living satisfying lives. They can keep you on track.

And resist the temptation to spend your time together complaining about your troubles. Stay in the moment and enjoy the company. You will emerge lighter and fortified to handle obstacles with courage and grace.

Stop Catastrophizing

Mind your story. Pay attention to the messages you are telegraphing yourself. "I can't get through this." "I hate my spouse." "I will end up homeless."

The way to subside worry is by not giving it center stage. Take the focus off the obstacles posed by the divorce and redirect your attention to possibility.

- You are blessed with a superb opportunity to rewrite your story. Every time a nasty thought pops up, make it your intention to replace it with one that serves you. How about:
- "This too, shall pass."
- "I am going through a bumpy ride right now, but I will arrive safely at my destination."
- "It is always darkest before dawn."
- "When this is over things will fall into place."
- "I am creating the awesome life I deserve."

You will always have dark nights of the soul. Remember that the sun will rise again. As will you.

Don't Break Down— Break Through! Keeping Your Focus at Work

A divorce is a life-altering event and, inevitably, there will be times when you'll feel overwhelmed by situations seemingly out of your control.

You had a heated argument with your spouse over who keeps the house and are seething with anger. Perhaps the judge denied your request to take the children to see your parents out of state. Or you feel overwhelmed by the divorce and fear you'll never have your life back.

Keeping your composure, focus and productivity at work may be difficult when your mind is consumed by worry, anger, and balancing multiple obligations for an extended and uncertain period of time.

So, keeping your focus on your work will be essential. After all, a steady income is key to preserving your financial solvency and quality of life, as well as your children's. Now is not the time to make mistakes, getting fired and being in the pickle of having to find another job.

This is not easy. I know it for a fact.

I divorced during my last semester in law school. Not only did I need to focus on my brain-taxing work as a court interpreter, I also had to go to school at night, write papers and move out of my house. Then there was the bar exam four months later.

It was daunting!

With so much on my plate, I thought I would burst at the seams; but my only choice was to go through it.

You can do it, too! As Winston Churchill said, "If you're going through hell, keep going."

The secret to "hell travel" is focusing on solutions: developing and implementing strategies to solve problems, whether at hand or expected, instead of catastrophizing worst-case scenarios or burying your head in the sand.

My success strategy consisted of keeping a structured schedule. I prioritized my responsibilities and allocated specific periods of time to individual tasks while maintaining my attention and focus.

Alternating tasks that used different skills or required various degrees of attention helped reduce mental fatigue.

And committing blocks of time for enjoyable activities between demanding tasks allowed me to keep my spirits up as I tried to juggle multiple commitments.

Use this strategy and stay productive and on schedule!

Take turns between engrossing and mindless tasks. Tidy up and organize your workspace after sitting at your desk for hours of brain-frying work. Clear your in-box. Or squeeze in something that feels good, like making calls to customers or colleagues you like. Tackle a research project that piques your curiosity and stimulates your mind.

Whatever helps you feel centered, balanced and on purpose, just do it.

And don't forget basking in healthy doses of TLC. When facing the stresses of divorce, a little support—from yourself and others—will go a long way.

Reach out to a trusted friend or mentor who will empower you while protecting your privacy and confidentiality. Tap into resources available through your employer, such as an Employee Assistance Program. Your therapist can also prove invaluable in helping you maintain your productivity and confidence.

As I struggled to finish my last semester in school and prepare for the bar exam, I had weekly meetings with a psychology graduate student at Rutgers University. She was the cheerleader whose warm smile and confidence in me inspired me to keep going, even when my strength was waning and my faith was put to the test.

Find someone reliable who can do the same for you.

Safeguarding Your Emotional Balance

Besides time management and staying focused, unsavory situations and challenges will test your patience and shake your composure.

You will need a plan to deal with them successfully.

I have already provided you with tools to help you manage stress levels and mood. But some things bear repeating and applying to the workplace context.

Figure out what situations seem to throw you off when you're trying to perform at work. Anticipate the problems you will probably encounter and put in place an action plan that incorporates quick-relief techniques. And be ready to deploy them on command.

Here are some possible scenarios:

- Does your soon-to-be ex get a thrill out of picking fights just before bedtime or before you go to work? Especially when you have an important meeting or presentation first thing in the morning?
- Does your lawyer call you at work to share unpleasant news when you should be on top of your game?
- Do feelings of worry take over your mind when you're handling a complex task?

Avoid upsetting events at inopportune times with these coping strategies:

- Agree with your lawyer not to call you to discuss non-emergent matters during your working hours. Lawyers usually work long days.
- Have your assistant (or voicemail) screen your calls to avoid upsetting conversations before an important deadline, meeting or presentation, or when you're performing a task that requires concentration or may

jeopardize your safety. If you mistakenly pick up a surprise call, politely excuse yourself unless it's urgent. Offer to return the call at a more convenient time.

- Consistently practice the exercises in this book and identify those that help you the most in specific situations. For example, if an argument with your spouse or a conversation with your lawyer steals your peace, practice active awareness. Notice the emerging negative thoughts and feelings and nip them in the bud before they get out of control.
- Stay in tune with the sensations in your body.
- Take a brisk walk at lunchtime to clear negative energy that is stuck in your body.
- Meditate for a few minutes and clear your head before tackling a difficult task.
- Repeat positive affirmations when you're overcome by negativity and self-doubt. Even better, do it throughout the day, between tasks and on breaks.
- B-R-E-A-T-H-E.

A Loving Warning

Burying yourself with work may seem like a smart idea. While it's good to keep busy, using work as a numbing mechanism may backfire if it prevents you from facing issues and emotions that you need to tackle head-on.

The same applies to addiction to any other activities and substances if used to avoid confronting your challenges.

Dependency and despondency will dig you deeper into the hole.

Instead, give yourself a reasonable time period to *feel and process* your emotions without dwelling on them. Set a timer for five to 10 minutes to release steam, vent and when the timer goes off, *move on.* Literally! Take a quick brisk walk or stretch to shake off the negative energy from your body. Now, back to work!

Remember, life unfolds one moment at a time. You *can* get through this moment, then the next moment, and the one after that.

Performing your best at work promotes a sense of accomplishment and increases your feelings of self-worth at this critical time.

Success is your birthright, and you were born to thrive. Step up and claim it!

PART V

CREATING THE HAPPINESS YOU DESERVE

Transcending Your Fears
and Writing a New Story

You may have felt trapped in an unhappy relationship, possibly out of fear, as we discussed earlier. These fears are natural in the face of uncertainty. And uncertainty is a fact of life. But unless you make peace with your fears, you will continue living an unsatisfactory life—even after your marriage ends—denying yourself of your right to be happy and free. You can transcend these fears and start creating a joyful life from scratch.

Fears are a mechanism built in to protect us, to keep us safe and away from danger. Fears provide an important service. But unfounded, irrational fears do not serve us, and we cannot allow them to run our lives.

When unchecked, fears enslave us. They paralyze us. They keep us stuck and prevent us from taking the actions that can improve our lives. They rob us of our peace. A mind cluttered with fearful thoughts is convinced of the certainty of a negative outcome and cannot see the light at the end of the tunnel. It is immune to logic, intuition and right action.

Despite their harmful effects, do not see your fears as enemies. Your fears have something to teach you. They have a message for you. And you will never receive that message if you resist or run away from your fears.

Carl Jung got it right when he said that what you resist persists. By fighting your fears, you are increasing their power over you. Instead, you want to *transcend* your fears. Make peace with them. Loosen their grip on you. Let them go the same way a child stops playing with a toy that is no longer appropriate for its age. With detachment.

The best way to transcend fear is to face it—head-on. To transcend fear, you need to stay with it. Spot it. Name it. Feel it in your body. And let it pass until it loses its power over you.

Ask yourself, "What is the worst thing that can happen?" Play the worst-case scenario in your head in all its gory details. As you repeat this routine over and over again, your fears will lose power over you. You will come to realize that most of your fears are baseless and are unlikely to materialize. Or that you have what it takes to find solutions and overcome your challenges successfully.

You can take it a step further and make your scene so ridiculous and implausible that it will make you laugh.

Once you have dissolved your fears, replace them with an alternative scenario that thrills you. Instead of fearing a future of loneliness and lack, change the script. See yourself succeeding, living in abundance, surrounded by love—from family, friends, a loving partner. The right one this time. It's your story. You can create it any way you want.

Release your fears and replace your faith in negative outcomes with the certainty that all is well. Once you convince yourself that your fears are unfounded, you will live fearlessly and freely.

Fear Release Exercise

Befriend your fear. Have a chat with it. Quiet your mind. Bring up your fears, one at a time. Ask each fear: "What are you trying to teach me? What is your message for me?" Then let the answers come to you. You may have an insight, or a phrase or image will come to mind. Pay attention and listen to what your fear is trying to say. Then you can speak to your fear: "I see you. Thank you for caring. Thank you for trying to protect me. But I can take it from here." Take a deep breath and release it. And live fearlessly.

Creating Your Future from the Inside Out

Now that you're cruising the high road to divorce and have adopted practices to empower yourself, it's time to get ready for the future. Let's start looking forward to a new life—a new you!

Begin imagining your life as you want it to be post-divorce. This is the *fun* part of the process. With the powers of imagination and determination, you can start to feel the joy of living your new life right here, right now, and bring the forces of the Universe to conspire to make your fondest dreams a reality.

As you practice these exercises, you will notice changes in your attitude and synchronicities everywhere. Little miracles will happen all around you. You will feel as though the world is on your side, cheering for you!

Harnessing the Power of Imagination

Your imagination is your most precious gift. Your most powerful ally. Maybe up to this point it has brought you undesirable conditions, and you have manifested the disaster you've been dreading all along. Now is the time to turn your imagination in your favor.

Imagination is that faculty of the mind where possibility exists, untethered, awaiting expression. In your imagination, anything is possible, without limitation. Imagination is that quality we all had as children, when we could be or do anything we could conceive with no regard for obstacles or "reality."

Ask any child what they want to be when they grow up, and their answers will run the gamut. The little boy who wants to be an astronaut is not bound by the limitations—real or imagined—that we, as adults, inflict on ourselves. This little boy is not thinking, "I need to be super smart, or go to college, get an advanced degree, go through grueling training and intense competition. I don't have the smarts, the money or the patience, so I might as well give up now." No, this child sees himself on the moon, conquering the universe, in utter delight.

Unfortunately, as we grow up, the adults in our lives taint our minds with "reality" and crush the imagination that could have propelled us to the moon and beyond. Instead, they poisoned creative minds with limiting beliefs of why we can't do what our hearts call us to do. We renounce our dreams and convert our workshop of possibility into a catastrophe factory.

Most likely your imagination has not been serving you up to now. You might have been using it to feed your fears and anxieties, predicting the worst. You may be telling yourself: "Things will never change. I will never be happy. If I leave my spouse, I will end up alone and homeless eating cat food under a bridge."

That's understandable, and you're in good company. We all do it. Experiencing fear is what our minds do best. It is essential to our survival. If we don't exercise caution, we might engage in dumb behaviors that would prematurely push us out of the gene pool.

But the good news is that your mind is yours and yours alone, and you have complete power to identify and deactivate your fear-based negative thinking. You can *choose* to create deliberately by engaging your imagination. Regardless of your circumstances—rich, poor, unhappily married or uneducated—you are gifted with unlimited potential to retrain your mind and to manifest whatever you desire.

This may sound like total woo woo, especially when you feel overwhelmed by marital miseries. It may be hard to conceive feeling free again, loving again. You are probably fixated on the negatives. And there might be many—at this time. But that can easily change through the exercise of your imaginary powers.

Ponder this… every human invention you see started out as an idea in someone's mind. Airplanes and helicopters are not the evolutionary siblings of the birds but were birthed in someone's imagination. And your mind possesses just as much power to bring creation into the world.

Once you understand that everything you see is the child of an idea, you can intentionally disregard your limiting programming and use your powerful imagination to create for yourself a future of bliss ahead. Imagination is the training camp where you practice your new life before you experience the real thing. Dreams and hopes are raw materials, and realization is the output.

Imagine and bring about the life of your dreams!

Visualization

Visualization is the most powerful way to harness the power of imagination to create your life intentionally. It enables you to bring about what you wish to experience. Visualization has increased in popularity in recent years, but it is not a new idea. For decades, it has been used by athletes and astronauts to simulate conditions, rehearse their moves and improve their performance. It has also been used by people like you and me to create their outer experiences with excellent results.

While it might seem mysterious, visualization works because the mind cannot tell the difference between what's real and what's imagined. And the subconscious mind, in its unlimited wisdom, will pool together the resources necessary to bring to pass what you've seen in your imagination.

Visualizing is simply using your mind's eye to imagine what you'd like to experience on the outside, with the unwavering expectation that it will come to pass. It is this simple:

- Close your eyes.
- Vividly picture yourself in your new life, doing the things you want, having the things you desire.
- Feel the emotions you'd feel when these desires become your reality.
- Feel grateful for receiving your wishes.

The key is to passionately bask in the emotions you will feel when your desire is fulfilled.

As a soon-to-be-free agent, picture in your mind the improved *you* that will come out of this journey. What do you look like? How do you spend your time?

Imagine yourself free and fulfilled pursuing new hobbies or successfully performing your amazing job or running your successful business. Relax in your gorgeous new home. Decorate it in your mind. Swim in your pool and feel the warmth of the sun as you taste your ice-cold margaritas. Take your children to their new school and have fun meeting their new friends, playing games or making them snacks. Whatever makes *you* happy—*imagine* it, *feel* it, *live* it!

Best-selling author and coach, Jennifer Grace, incorporates epic music in her visualization meditation to add power and emotion. She recommends engaging all the senses, not just your vision, to amplify the effects of the visualization practice.

For best results, visualization must be done consistently. Practice at least twice a day, when you wake up in the morning and before you go to bed. Visualizing in the morning will set the stage for a fruitful day, while bedtime visualizing will feed to your subconscious mind your innermost desires and benefit from your relaxed state to create your tomorrow. Visualizing right after meditation, when your mind is quiet, is a fantastic way to magnify the effects of your visualization practice.

The Vision Board: The Ultimate Visual Aid

A vision board is an easy way to put visualization to work and get you started, especially if it doesn't come naturally to you. A vision board is a bulletin board, poster or screen where you attach pictures that represent your desires—material or intangible—and inspirational words that pump you up every time you look at it.

An effective vision board is more than just clippings of pictures of things you'd like to own. The vision board reminds you of your intention and is designed to evoke in you the feelings of having achieved those desires.

Go through magazines or books and cut out pictures of things you want to attract or that elicit the feelings you wish to experience. You can include clippings of your ideal home, dream vacation or extreme sport. It can be your face attached to a body in your ideal shape or donning the most fabulous outfit in the world. Perhaps it is a picture of a climber reaching the summit, beaming on top of the world.

Cut out words and phrases that inspire you, wise quotes and affirmations, and paste them next to the corresponding images. Look at your vision board often, experiencing the feelings of joy and gratitude for receiving the desires represented by your vision board.

Creating a vision board is easy and lots of fun. Go wild! There are plenty of aids out there to help you create the vision board that's perfect for you. With so many apps available to create a vision board on your computer, tablet or phone, you can stay inspired anywhere, anytime.

For a profound, soul-searching experience, check out the book *Visioning: Ten Steps to Designing the Life of Your Dreams* by expressive arts therapist Lucia Capacchione. It presents a roadmap to the creative process that you can apply to various areas of your life, such as relationships, career, home and prosperity, to help you bring forth your dreams into physical reality. I used this book to create my first vision boards and delighted in the journey of personal exploration.

Whatever method you choose, creating a vision board should evoke feelings of excitement, joy and unlimited possibility. In essence, a roadmap of your life, the way you want it.

And don't limit yourself to a few moments of scheduled visualization. Practice visualization at every opportunity—in the shower, having breakfast, at the supermarket checkout line. Use every available minute of your day—and night—to create the life of your dreams.

And remember, if you're going to dream, dream big. No dream is too big. No dream is more than what you deserve. Because you deserve to be happy.

Reflections
With the power of your imagination on your
side, grab your journal and do the exercises
below to help you bring about a
new life of freedom and fulfillment.

Freedom

What is your personal definition of freedom? Is it living on
your own? Financial security? Making your own decisions and
following your passions? Working from home? Having more time
to pursue your passions? A peaceful mind?
In what ways do your marital troubles
prevent you from feeling free?
What things do you need to release in order to feel free?
What do you need to attract into your life to feel free?
Make a list of all the things that would
increase your feelings of freedom.
Visualize yourself enjoying this freedom for
five minutes every morning and five minutes before bed.
Add pictures to represent these goals to your vision board.
Make a list of steps you can take to make it happen for you.
Tap into your intuition for insights.
Take action on one item from your list each day.

Fulfillment

What is your personal ideal of fulfillment?
Is it rewarding relationships? Succeeding at your career?

Expressing your talents and creativity? Living on purpose?
Spiritual development? Volunteering for a
cause you feel passionate about?
What is missing from your life that
would make you feel fulfilled?
Do you believe your marriage has interfered
with your attaining fulfillment? How?
In what ways have you stopped yourself
from pursuing fulfilling endeavors?
Make a list of accomplishments that
would make you feel fulfilled.
If you find it useful, break down your answers by categories, such
as personal time, family, career, health and fitness, or any other
areas that are key to your self-realization.
Visualize yourself achieving these goals for five minutes every
morning and five minutes before bed.
Add pictures to represent these goals to your vision board.
Make a list of steps you can take to achieve these goals.
Tap into your intuition for insights.
Take action on one item from your list each day.

Like happiness, freedom and fulfillment are states of mind. Like happiness, they are your personal responsibility, and only you can bring them to fruition. Make freedom and fulfillment the pillars of your personal happiness project and delight in the process of deliberate creation.

Will You Love Again?

One pressing question in the minds of people who are miserably married or going through divorce is, "Will I be loved again?"

Fear of not finding love again may keep you hostage in an unsatisfying marriage. It may haunt you if your spouse has abandoned you.

It is normal to feel sad and lonely and to crave an intimate connection with a partner. Especially when you have been rejected or regret wasting your "best years" in a toxic marriage.

So, naturally, marital woes will heighten your anxiety about being loved, and the fear of not hanging on to love may lead you to doubt your lovability or your capacity to love.

We all want to be loved. We were created to be and express love.

Make no mistake. *We are all loving and lovable.* And that includes you.

If you're no spring chicken, you will factor age in your desirability equation and conclude that dating or remarrying is not in your cards.

However, your capacity to express and receive love knows no bounds or age limits. It is not predetermined by your past experiences. It is merely *suppressed* by your negative thinking.

People in all age groups rebuild their lives and enjoy fulfilling relationships. The pool of candidates doesn't necessarily shrink. In fact, it expands as potential mates lose their partners to divorce or death.

Don't go into self-isolation, barricading yourself from romance. Avoid replaying in your head stories of rejection, anger and betrayal. Hating and bashing members of the opposite sex assuming they are all the same is counterproductive. Do not invite into your life self-fulfilling prophesies of destruction and doom. You can rebuild your life from where you are right now and attract a new partner and a joyous relationship.

On the other hand, resist the temptation to hook up right away. Be over your ex first. Reflect upon the reasons why you got married, and make sure that none of the factors that lured you into the wrong marriage will lead you to a disaster do-over.

When Is it Okay to Date Again?

There is no *right time* to start dating. But there's definitely a *wrong time* and plenty of *wrong reasons* to recouple.

Here are some particularly bad ones:

- You feel lonely or incomplete.
- You want to numb your pain.
- You're afraid you can't survive on your own.
- You need a partner to prove your desirability.
- You want a partner to help you get over your ex.
- You want to make your ex jealous.

You may be entertaining some of these thoughts or feelings and wonder what is wrong with that. While you need to honor and process your emotions, you cannot allow them to run your love life. Doing so is a recipe for disaster that guarantees failure.

Ensuring that you are ready to date will prime you for a successful relationship and prevent you from recycling the mistakes of your past.

Your Point of Attraction

Let's start with some basics. You've surely heard the expression "Like attracts like," and "Misery loves company." These statements are spot on. They reveal the mechanism by which we attract everything, including partners.

How you think and feel creates your point of attraction. It determines the kind of companion that will be drawn to you. And this is not "woo woo." It is plain common sense.

If you are constantly complaining and feeling sorry for yourself, you can only attract a pity-party animal. And if you speak of nothing other than your ex, you will attract an emotionally unavailable individual who is not over his or her ex either. An emotionally healthy person would run away from you in a New York minute.

Likewise, dating from a point of weakness, while harboring hatred and resentment, will generate an unhealthy point of attraction that will invite a partner who is a mirror image of your insecurities and negative emotions.

If you have children, you must exercise sound judgment and be especially cautious about bringing new lovers home. Exposing your children to a partner with a criminal history, mental health problems or substance abuse issues may hurt you in a custody battle.

Thus, tending to your emotional health and releasing all your attachments to your marriage is the key to a fresh start.

Revisit the reflections from previous chapters for useful insights.

Love Yourself First If You Want to Be Loved by Others

Your desirability stems from self-love. Marital problems have probably wounded, not only the love in your marriage, but your love for yourself. Rejection, put downs, abusive or inconsiderate behaviors from your spouse may have led you to question your lovability.

Ironically, the feelings of high you experience in a new relationship and that you may crave now come from within, not from a partner. I know that may seem inconceivable *at this time but* bear with me.

That idea hit me like a ton of bricks when I read the book *Secrets About Life Every Woman Should Know: Ten Principles for Total Emotional and Spiritual Fulfillment* by Barbara De Angelis. In it, De Angelis describes the elation she enjoyed in a romantic relationship, only to find out that the man she was madly in love with was cheating on her.

She wondered how she could feel so blissful when this man was not in love with her. This experience made De Angelis realize that all the love and ecstasy she was perceiving could not have flowed from this man—they came from within herself.

Become the love you want to receive. To achieve that, you must first love yourself. Make nurturing yourself a priority. Only then can you be ripe to love and be loved by another.

Creating an exciting single life is another strategy to prepare for successful recoupling. Fill your life with people—friends and family—and activities that bring you joy. Learn to enjoy your own company. Get comfortable with solitude, too, and free yourself from your dependence on others for security or entertainment.

Regain your confidence and rebuild your life from a position of personal power using the strategies offered in this book. Radiating love and joy will turn you into an irresistible magnet to healthy individuals, and, potentially, to a new partner.

It is then time to go out in the world and share your life and the love you have become with someone who deserves you.

Reflections
What feelings impulse your desire to date?
Loneliness? A desire to share?
Is dating a way to prove your desirability—
to yourself? Your ex? Others?
What are you seeking from a partner?
Do you love yourself?
Do you enjoy your own company?
How can you make your time
alone more enjoyable?
What do you bring into a relationship
with a romantic partner?

Divorce from Your Spouse, Not to Your Spouse

Your divorce judgment has been signed and filed with the court, and you think it is finally OVER.

Is it?

That's entirely up to you.

You have a choice to be forever divorced "from your spouse" or to be divorced "to your spouse" in perpetuity. Divorcing *from* your spouse means moving on freely and leaving relationship baggage behind. Divorcing *to* your spouse means clinging to your emotional entanglements, simmering in anger and resentment.

What will it be?

You know you are divorced from your ex when:

- You have forgiven your spouse for all wrongs, real or perceived.
- You have acknowledged your role in the demise of your marriage.

- You have forgiven yourself and made amends for your transgressions.
- You have let go of attachments to all dreams, hopes and expectations you held regarding marriage in general and your spouse in particular.
- You have let go of grudges, resentments and ill feelings.
- You stop thinking frequently about your spouse.
- You search for and digest the lessons offered by the relationship.
- You feel gratitude for the experience.

Conversely, you are divorced *to* your ex when:

- You hold on to grudges.
- You refuse to forgive.
- You entertain thoughts of revenge.
- You hope for reconciliation after your marriage is over.
- You ask your children to spy for you on your ex's life, activities and new partners.
- You obsess about your spouse and spy on him or her on social media or intentionally post to engender jealousy.
- You disparage your ex with your children and sabotage their relationship.
- You unreasonably interfere with or deprive your ex of parenting time.
- You plot and execute ways to punish your ex.
- You take your spouse to court at every opportunity.

- You constantly think about your ex and talk about him or her with anyone who will listen.

Don't kid yourself. When you remain divorced to your spouse, you are not hurting your ex. You are hurting your children. And you are hurting yourself.

Being divorced to your spouse will keep you imprisoned. You will experience neither peace or freedom. Attachment to an old relationship limits your possibility to enter into healthy new relationships and bond with a new partner. You can't truly connect with a new partner if you're still feeling negative emotions or unrequited love for your ex.

Only when you divorce from your spouse you are free to live and love again. You can create your future life on a clean slate. Give yourself another chance to be happy.

If you find yourself unable to move forward, keep this book handy and repeat the exercises in it to help you release yourself. Reflect daily and journal often. Seek support from friends and family and, if necessary, a professional counselor.

May you find the healing you deserve. *Because you deserve to be happy!*

Moving On Is the Best Revenge

As you finish reading this book, I sincerely hope that it has been a supportive companion on your personal journey. I hope it has been awakening and illuminating. It is my greatest desire that you are now living a life bursting with freedom, fulfillment and limitless joy. That you are radiating empowerment and confidence.

Remember, divorce is about getting on with your life, not about getting even. Stay on course, creating the life you deserve, because you deserve to be happy.

The journey of life is not over till it's over. This is just the beginning of a marvelous adventure. Continue with your empowering practices, nurture your spirit and stay in touch. I would love to hear from you!

My loving thoughts and support are with you always. Peace!

Before You Say Goodbye

Beloved Reader,

Help me spread the fantastic news of unlimited possibility for all!

If you liked the book as much as I enjoyed writing it for you, it would mean the world to me if you left a review and shared it with others who may benefit the way you have.

Thank you for reading and joy to you always!

About the Author

Sonia Frontera is a divorce lawyer with a heart. She is the survivor of a toxic marriage who is now happily remarried.

Sonia integrates the wisdom acquired through her personal journey, her professional experience and the lessons of the world's leading transformational teachers and translates it into guidance that is insightful and practical. She is a Certified Canfield Success Principles Trainer.

Through the years, Sonia has supported domestic violence survivors as an advocate, speaker and empowerment trainer.

She is a compulsive knitter who is happiest hanging out in her country home with her husband and their three street-dogs-turned-princesses.

Contact Sonia

Sonia loves to hear from readers. Visit her internet home at
https://www.soniafrontera.com

Works and Resources Cited

"Adding Physical Activity to Your Life." Centers for Disease Control and Prevention (website). Updated April 30, 2020, www.cdc.gov/physicalactivity/basics/adding-pa/index.htm.

Association of Family Conciliation Courts (website). Accessed June 6, 2020, www.afccnet.org.

"2016 Annual Relationship, Marriage, and Divorce Survey, Final Report." Avvo (website). Accessed June 6, 2020, marketing-assets.avvo.com/uploads/sites/3/2016/05/Avvo-Relationship-Study_Final-Research-Report.pdf?_ga=1.11109 5629.91601001.1442439306.

"FAQ for Meditation." Tara Brach (website). Accessed June 6, 2020, www.tarabrach.com/faq-for-meditation2.

"Guided Meditations." Tara Brach (website). Accessed June 6, 2020, www.tarabrach.com/guided-meditations.

Canfield, Jack and Mark Victor Hansen. *Chicken Soup for the Soul: 101 Stories to Open the Heart and Rekindle the Spirit.* Boca Raton: Health Communications, Inc., 1993.

Canfield, Jack and Janet Switzer. *The Success Principles™ - 10th Anniversary Edition: How to Get from Where You Are to Where You Want to Be.* New York: Harper Collins, 2015.

Capacchione, Lucia. *Visioning: Ten Steps to Designing the Life of Your Dreams.* New York: Penguin Publishing Group, 2000.

Daily Word, Unity Village (MO): Unity, 2020.

De Angelis, Barbara. *Secrets About Life Every Woman Should Know: Ten Principles for Total Emotional and Spiritual Fulfillment.* New York: Hyperion, 1999.

De Mello, Anthony. *Awareness: A de Mello Spirituality Conference in His Own Words.* New York: Image Books, 1992.

Emery, Robert. *The Truth About Children and Divorce.* New York: Penguin Group USA, 2006.

Gaines, Edwene. *The Four Spiritual Laws of Prosperity: A Simple Guide to Unlimited Abundance.* Emmaus (PA): Rodale, 2005.

"Get Better Sleep." American Sleep Association (website). Accessed June 6, 2020, www.sleepassociation.org/about-sleep/get-better-sleep.

Gillard, Jemma. "Do YOU Regret Getting Divorced? Astonishing 50 Per Cent of People Wish They Had Never Ended Their Marriage." *Daily Mail*, August 18, 2014, www.dailymail.co.uk/femail/article-2727716/Is-going-separate-ways-really-good-idea-Astonishing-50-divorcees-regret-breaking-partner.html?printingPage=true.

Hawkins, David R. *In the World but not of It: Living Spiritually in the Modern World.* Nightingale Conant, 2008. Audiobook, 6 CDs.

Hay, Louise. *You Can Heal Your Life.* Santa Monica (CA): Hay House, 1987.

Hay, Louise and Cheryl Richardson. *You Can Trust Your Life.* Hay House, 12/17/12. 4-DVD Set.

Hetherington, E. Mavis and John Kelly. *For Better or For Worse: Divorce Reconsidered.* New York: W. W. Norton & Company, 2003.

Ilibagiza, Immaculee. *Left to Tell: Discovering God in the Midst of the Rwandan Holocaust.* Carlsbad (CA): Hay House, 2014.

Montenegro, Xenia P. "The Divorce Experience: A Study of Divorce at Midlife and Beyond." Washington, DC: AARP Research, May 2004, doi.org/10.26419/res.00061.001.

"Path to Safety." The National Domestic Violence Hotline (website). Accessed June 6, 2020, www.thehotline.org/help/path-to-safety.

"Physical Activity and Health." Centers for Disease Control and Prevention (website). Accessed June 6, 2020, https://www.cdc.gov/physicalactivity/.

Progoff Intensive Journal® Program for Self-Development (website). Accessed June 6, 2020, www.intensivejournal.org.

"Psychological Benefits of Exercise." Association for Applied Sports Psychology (website). Accessed June 6, 2020, www.appliedsportpsych.org/resources/health-fitness-resources/psychological-benefits-of-exercise.

Richardson, Cheryl. *The Art of Extreme Self-Care: Transform Your Life One Month at a Time.* Carlsbad (CA): Hay House, 2012.

Sedona Method (website). Accessed June 6, 2020, www.sedona.com

Sex and the City. Directed by Michael Patrick King, HBO Films, 2008.

Sister Stan. *Gardening the Soul: Mindful Thoughts and Meditations for Every Day of the Year.* Dublin: Transworld Ireland, 2017.

Stepler, Renee. "Led by Baby Boomers, Divorce Rates Climb for America's 50+ Population." *Pew Research Center*, March 9, 2017,

www.pewresearch.org/fact-tank/2017/03/09/led-by-baby-boomers-divorce-rates-climb-for-americas-50-population.

Taylor, Terry Lynn and Mary Beth Crain. *Angel Wisdom: 365 Meditations and Insights from the Heavens.* New York: Harper Collins, 1994.

Tipping, Colin. *Radical Forgiveness: Making Room for the Miracle.* Louisville (CO): Sounds True, 2010.

Vanzant, Iyanla. *Forgiveness: 21 Days to Forgive Everyone for Everything.* Carlsbad (CA): SmileyBooks, 2013.

Weil, Andrew, M.D. *Breathing: The Master Key to Self-Healing.* Louisville (CO): Sounds True, 1999. Audio CD.

Weil™Andrew Weil, M.D.(website), Healthy Lifestyle Brands, L.L.C. Accessed June 6, 2020, www.drweil.com.

Weil, Andrew, M.D. *Spontaneous Healing: How to Discover and Enhance Your Body's Natural Ability to Maintain and Heal Itself.* New York: Fawcett Columbine, 1995, pp. 206-207.

Willoughby, Jennie. Interview with Anderson Cooper. Anderson Cooper 360. CNN. 8 February 2018.

Women's Institute for Financial Education (website). Accessed June 6, 2020, www.wife.org.

Unchained at Last (website). Accessed June 6, 2020, https://www.unchainedatlast.org/.

Domestic Violence Resources

United States
The National Domestic Violence Hotline
www.thehotline.org
Tel: 800 799-7233

Australia
ReachOut.com
Tel: 1800 RESPECT
If you're in immediate danger dial 000.

Canada
Canada Department of Justice
www.justice.gc.ca
For emergency help dial 9-1-1 or contact your local police
emergency number.

England
Refuge
www.refuge.org.uk
Women's Aid Federation
www.womensaid.org.uk
Joint Freephone: 0808 2000247

Ireland
Safe Ireland
www.safeireland.ie

<u>Women's Aid</u>
www.womensaid.ie
Joint National Freephone Domestic Violence Helpline: 1800 341 900

New Zealand
<u>Ministry of Health</u>
www.health.govt.nz

<u>Women's Refuge</u>
www.womensrefuge.org.nz
For emergency help dial 111 or 0800 REFUGE.

Scotland
<u>Citizens Advice Scotland</u>
www.citizensadvice.org.uk/scotland

Wales
<u>Live Fear Free</u>
livefearfree.gov.wales
Live Fear Free Helpline: 0808 8010 800
Call 999 if you or someone you know is in immediate danger.

<u>Welsh Women's Aid</u>
www.womensaid.org.uk
Helpline: 0808 2000 247

arrangements to have friends or family members be available to assist you or stay with you.

Speak to a therapist and get professional advice before you have this delicate conversation. The National Domestic Violence Hotline can also help you plan your safe escape.

Now that you've dropped the "D Bomb," let the mushroom cloud settle, and give yourself a chance to collect yourself before you continue on your journey.

Charting the Escape Route

Setting the Pace

This is *your* divorce. Only you can decide what's best for you— and that includes the timing of your separation. There are no rules dictating how fast to go from wondering what to do to getting a divorce decree.

Be patient with yourself and focus on your needs, not on pleasing others or meeting their expectations, or feeling bound by imaginary deadlines. Don't let people push you to stay or to leave if you are not ready for the journey.

It took me years to sort through and overcome issues of faith, self-doubt and family opposition before I was emotionally prepared to go through the mystery of divorce. My self-image as "not a quitter" kept me from deciding fast enough, and I stayed married much longer than I should have.

But rather than blame myself, I *chose* to congratulate myself for taking action and unpacking the lessons that came from the years I spent with my ex-husband. I remained faithful to the possibility that life was unfolding in perfection, and that, even though I didn't understand why it took me so long, in the end everything would be fine. And I was right.

The key is advancing step by step towards self-empowerment. Pause to reflect on your progress, making sure you're not clinging on to the hope of the impossible or that you're living in denial, with an unrealistic expectation that everything will fix itself on its own.

Be easy on yourself by taking baby steps towards your liberation. Drive around the neighborhood where you'd like to live. Look for listings of homes and rentals in that neighborhood. If you intend to stay at the same home, get rid of clutter and donate or sell items you won't need in your future life. Start decorating your "new" place and surround yourself with beautiful things that bring you joy.

Begin doing the things you would like to pursue when you are free at last. Enroll in courses that are fun or pursue those activities your spouse would not do with you. The Universe loves determination and will support your agenda— if you get started! Take inspiration from Lao Tzu's wisdom: "The journey of a thousand miles begins with one step." Take it now!

Reflections
Do frequent check-ins. Are you
making progress or are you in denial?
If you find it helpful, make a list of targets
you'd like to complete to get to the finish line.
Prepare a timeline with estimated completion
dates and reward yourself for each
accomplishment, no matter how small.